THE RATIONALE DIVINORUM OFFICIORUM
OF WILLIAM DURAND OF MENDE

RECORDS OF WESTERN CIVILIZATION

Records of Western Civilization is a series published under the auspices of the Interdepartmental Committee on Medieval and Renaissance Studies of the Columbia University Graduate School. The Western Records are, in fact, a new incarnation of a venerable series, the Columbia Records of Civilization, which, for more than half a century, published sources and studies concerning great literary and historical landmarks. Many of the volumes of that series retain value, especially for their translations into English of primary sources, and the Medieval and Renaissance Studies Committee is pleased to cooperate with Columbia University Press in reissuing a selection of those works in paperback editions, especially suited for classroom use, and in limited clothbound editions.

COMMITTEE FOR THE RECORDS OF WESTERN CIVILIZATION

TIMOTHY M. THIBODEAU

THE RATIONALE DIVINORUM

OFFICIORUM OF WILLIAM

DURAND OF MENDE

{ *A New Translation of the Prologue and Book One* }

COLUMBIA UNIVERSITY PRESS   NEW YORK

Columbia University Press
Publishers Since 1893
New York   Chichester, West Sussex
Copyright © 2007
Columbia University Press
All rights reserved

Library of Congress Cataloging-in-Publication Data

Durand, Guillame, ca. 1230–1296.
[Rationale divinorum officiorum. Prologue. English]
The rationale divinorum officiorum of William Durand of Mende : a new
translation of the prologue and book one / Timothy M. Thibodeau.
    p. cm. — (Records of Western civilization)
Includes bibliographical references (p.) and index.
ISBN 978-0-231-14180-2 (cloth : alk. paper) — ISBN 978-0-231-51221-3
(ebook)
    1. Christian art and symbolism.   2. Church architecture.   3. Symbolism in
architecture.   I. Thibodeau, T.M. (Timothy M.)   II. Durand,
Guillaume, ca. 1230–1296. Rationale divinorum officiorum.
Book   1. English.   III. Title.   IV. Series.

Bv150.D8   2007
246—dc22   2007018735

RECORDS OF WESTERN CIVILIZATION

CONTENTS

PREFACE

To the modern student of medieval liturgy, William Durand of Mende (c. 1230–1296) needs no introduction. But to those who are newcomers to the field of medieval studies, particularly at the undergraduate level, it is appropriate that I offer these words of explanation about Durand's invaluable contribution to our understanding of the medieval Christian worldview.

As I worked on the present volume, there was a media extravaganza for the premiere of the film version of Dan Brown's best-selling novel *The Da Vinci Code.* In a culture that has become increasingly visual, where images often eclipse spoken and written words, it is not surprising that Brown's fictional Professor Robert Langdon has such a strong appeal to the millions of fans of the book. Langdon is a "symbologist" sleuth who discovers that some of the most revered works of Western Christian art and architecture have thinly veiled secret messages that reveal the true identity of the Holy Grail. (His fictional grail is none other than Mary Magdalene, who supposedly settled in Provence and gave birth to Jesus' daughter.)

More than seven hundred years ago, another symbologist of a much different sort put pen to parchment and decoded a vastly different set of Christian mysteries: those that are embedded in the sacred spaces, rituals, and images of the Church. Unlike the fictional Robert Langdon, who lives in the modern secular culture of an Ivy League university, William Durand of Mende was the bishop of an impoverished diocese in Provence; he lived and ministered in a predominantly Christian society. As an interpreter and expositor of the "Divine Offices," or worship services of the Church, Durand was not out to "solve mysteries," in a

historical sense. The mysteries that he contemplates are not the historical puzzles from the past that consume Langdon but the timeless mysteries of faith that are ritually reenacted in the liturgies and devotional
practices of the Church.

Durand's sleuthing is therefore theological and spiritual. He has attempted, as he says in the general prologue of the *Rationale divinorum
officiorum*, to "unveil and explain as clearly as possible" the eternal truths
of salvation history, from the creation of the world to the future coming
of Christ. For medieval Christians, this sacred history was symbolically
brought to life every time they entered a church and contemplated its
physical structure and artwork; when they heard the church bells ringing; when they entered into one of the great liturgical seasons of the
Church; when they attended Mass; when they interred their dead.

The present treatise will strike the modern reader, so far removed
from Durand's cultural milieu, as odd and sometimes bizarre. But his
allegorical reading of the church building (as if it were a text) and the
liturgical activities that take place therein is precisely what his medieval
audience expected. As an allegorist, Durand stands squarely in a long
tradition of biblical exegesis that goes back to the early Church Fathers
whom he frequently quotes. For medieval authors, the "historical sense"
of Scripture was but one form of reading it (and for Durand, often the
least important). As he lucidly explains in his general prologue, the allegorical sense—where the bare text has a hidden or deeper meaning that
points to a higher truth—is best suited for grasping the rich symbolism
of the liturgy and the liturgical arts. Durand is not an innovator but a
compiler of a well-established tradition that stretches back from his era
to the Latin Fathers of the fifth and sixth centuries. This surely accounts
for the spectacular success of his lengthy exposition in his own day and
well beyond it.

It is my hope that the present volume will revive interest in the contribution of this French bishop to our comprehension of the entire medieval tradition of allegorical interpretation of the liturgy. The modern
student of medieval symbolism can find no surer or more complete
guide for the task of journeying through the sacred edifices, images, and
rituals of medieval Christendom than the "Rationale for the Divine Offices" of William Durand of Mende.

The preparation of this volume for publication would not have been
possible without the help and support of a number of people whom
I would like to thank. First, I must express my deep gratitude to John
Edelman, professor of philosophy at Nazareth College. John's skill as a

proofreader is matched by his appreciation of the difficulties of medieval Latin. He was kind enough to read and critique several chapters of this translation. My wife Susan offered her usual expert advice for important editorial changes to the structure of the introduction. Her suggestions have made the text more accessible to nonspecialists. A sabbatical grant from Nazareth College of Rochester for the spring 2006 semester provided a welcome space of time to review and edit the entire work before it went to press.

Finally, I would like to thank the many students whom I have been fortunate to have in my classes for the past eighteen years at Nazareth College. They have continually inspired me to achieve my best as a teacher, scholar, and mentor. This book is dedicated to them.

ABBREVIATIONS

COLLECTIONS OR EDITIONS

AHMA   G. M. Dreves, C. Blume and H. M. Bannister. *Analecta Hymnica Medii Aevi*, 55 vols. (Leipzig: O.R. Reisland, 1866–1922; repr., New York: Johnson Reprint, 1961)

AMS   R. J. Hesbert, *Antiphonale Missarum Sextuplex* (Bruselles: Vromant, 1935)

CAO   R. J. Hesbert, *Corpus Antiphonalium Officii*, 6 vols. and indices (Rome: Herder, 1963–1979)

CCCM   *Corpus Christianorum, Continuatio Mediaevalis* (Turnhout: Brepols Publishers, 1966–)

CCSL   *Corpus Christianorum, Series Latina* (Turnhout: Brepols Publishers, 1953–)

CSEL   *Corpus Scriptorum Ecclesiasticorum Latinorum* (Vienna: Vienna Academy, 1866–1957)

Deshusses Jean Deshusses, ed., *Le sacramentaire grégorien: Ses principales formes d'après les plus anciens manuscrits*, 2nd ed., Spicilegium Friburgense 16, 24, 28 (Fribourg: Éditions universitaires, 1979–1982)

Duchesne   Louis Duchesne, ed., *Le Liber Pontificialis*, 2nd ed., 3 vols. Bibliothèque des Écoles françaises d'Athènes et de Rome (Paris: E. de Boccard, 1955–1957)

Isidore, *Etym.* *Isidorus Hispalensis, Etymologiarum sive originum libri xx*, ed. W. M. Lindsay (Oxford: Oxford University Press, 1911; repr., Oxford: Oxford University Press, 1990)

Friedberg	Emile Friedberg, *Corpus Iuris Canonici*, 2 vols. (Leipzig: Bernard Tauchnitz, 1879; repr., Graz: Akademische Druck-u. Verlagsanstalt, 1959)
H	"Hadrianum," in Deshusses, *Le Sacramentaire grégorien: Ses principales formes d'après les plus anciens manuscrits*, vol. 1, 2nd ed., Spicilegium Friburgense 16 (Fribourg: Éditions universitaires, 1979)
Mommsen	Theodore Mommsen et al., *Corpus Iuris Civilis*, 3 vols. (Berlin: Weidmann, 1872–1895; repr., Hildesheim: Weidmann, 1988–1989)
OR	Michel Andrieu, ed., *Les Ordines Romani du haut Moyen Age*, 5 vols., Spicilegium Sacrum Lovaniense 11, 23, 24, 28, 29 (Louvain, 1931–1961)
OrdPC	S. J. P. Van Dijk and J. Hazeldon Walker, *The Ordinal of the Papal Court from Innocent III to Boniface VIII and Related Documents*, Spicilegium Friburgense 22 (Fribourg: University Press, 1975)
PG	J. P. Migne, ed., *Patrologia Graeca*, 2nd series (Paris, 1857–1866)
PL	J. P. Migne, ed., *Patrologia Latina* (Paris, 1844–1855); indices (Paris, 1862–1864)
PCR	Michel Andrieu, ed., *Le Pontifical Romain au Moyen Age II: Le Pontifical de la Curie Romaine*, Studi e Testi 87 (Vatican City: Bibiloteca Apostolica Vaticana, 1940)
PGD	Michel Andrieu, ed., *PRMA III: Le Pontifical de Guillaume Durand*, Studi e Testi 88 (Vatican City: Bibiloteca Apostolica Vaticana, 1940)
PRG	C. Vogel and R. Elze. *Le Pontifical romano- germanique du Xe siècle*, Studi e Testi 226, 227, 269 (Vatican City: Bibiloteca Apostolica Vaticana, 1963, 1972)
PRS12	Michel Andrieu, ed., *PRMA I: Le Pontifical romain du XIIe siècle*, Studi e Testi 86 (Vatican City: Biblioteca Apostolica Vaticana, 1938)
SC	*Sources Chrétiennes* (Paris: Éditions du Cerf, 1949–)
Sp	"Supplementum Anianense," in Deshusses, *Le Sacramentaire Grégorien: Ses principales formes d'après les plus anciens manuscrits*, vol. 1, 2nd ed., Spicilegium Friburgense 16 (Fribourg: Éditions universitaires, 1979)
Vulg.	Robert Weber and Boniface Fischer, eds. *Biblia Sacra iuxta Vulgatam Versionem*, 3rd ed. (Stuttgart: Deutsche Bibelgesellschaft, 1983)

JURIDICAL SOURCES

Decretum Gratiani (Friedberg 1)

D.1 c.1	Distinctio 1, capitulum 1
C.1 q.1 c.1	Causa 1, questio 1, capitulum 1
De pen.	Causa 33, questio 3 (De penitentia)
De cons.	Tractatus de consecratione
d.a.c.	Dictum Gratiani ante capitulum
d.p.c.	Dictum Gratiani post capitulum

Collectiones (Friedberg 2)

X 1.1.1	Decretales Gregorii IX (Liber Extra)
VI 1.1.1	Decretales Bonifacii VIII (Liber Sextus)

Corpus Iuris Civilis (Mommsen)

Cod. 1.1.1	Codex, lib.1, cap.1, par. 1
Dig.	Digesta
Inst.	Institutiones
Nou.	Nouellarum constitutiones (secundum Criticam)
Coll.	Ibid. (secundum Vulgatam)[1]

---

1. There are significant editorial and occasional textual differences between the classical text of this portion of the Roman law (*secundum Criticam*) and the medieval "Vulgate" (*secundum Vulgatam*) version that was used in the universities of Durand's day. These differences are duly noted in my references to Mommsen's edition of the classical text to show where the numbering differs between his edition and the medieval text.

INTRODUCTION

THE LIFE OF DURAND OF MENDE

William Durand[1] the Elder (c. 1230–1 Nov. 1296), bishop of Mende, France, was unquestionably the most renowned liturgical scholar of the later Middle Ages.[2] His variegated career path and impressive literary output are very much a reflection of the clerical, university culture of the thirteenth-century Roman Church. He was born in the village of Puimisson (c. 1230–31),[3] but we know virtually nothing about Durand's family or early life before he received clerical orders (c. 1250–55). His formal education began in the cathedral schools of Provence, and his academic program ended with a doctoral degree in canon law (c. 1260–63) from the premiere institution of his day for the study of jurisprudence, the University of Bologna. Durand's expertise as a jurist eventually earned him the moniker the "Speculator," since his mammoth textbook on procedural law, the *Speculum iudiciale* (c.1271–72)[4] or the "Mirror for magistrates," was quickly regarded as the definitive treatment of the subject among legal scholars of his era.

Within a few years of completing his studies in Bologna, Durand entered the service of the papal curia, where he remained for roughly the next two decades. His many years of curial service saw him advance from papal chaplain to increasingly difficult and onerous responsibilities, including his work as papal lawyer, diplomat, and official advisor for Pope Gregory X (r. 1271–1276) at the Second Council of Lyons (1274); he also played a key role in editing the official decrees of this general council.[5] Not surprisingly, the final years of his life were spent as a temporal ruler in warring papal territories during the tumultuous pontificate of his friend and confidant, Benedict Gaetani, or Pope Boniface VIII (r. 1294–1303).

Durand's long administrative career in Rome was temporarily inter-
rupted when he was elected bishop of Mende by the cathedral chapter
of his diocese in the spring of 1285. Though he received episcopal consecration from the archbishop of Ravenna in the fall of 1286, for inexpli-
cable reasons, Durand did not actually take up residence in Mende until
the summer of 1291. But the years of his episcopacy were precisely the
point where he turned with full vigor to the production of the numerous liturgical texts that ensured his lasting fame as the greatest liturgist
of the later Middle Ages. During that period, Durand redacted a *Liber
Ordinarium*[6] regulating the worship services of the cathedral of Mende;
he issued the *Constitutiones synodales* and *Instructiones*,[7] the first synodal statutes published for the clergy of his diocese; he completed his
magisterial *Pontificale* (c. 1295),[8] or "Bishop's book," which became the
definitive medieval pontifical—it was eventually adopted by the Roman
Curia and was unrivalled in the Latin Church until the liturgical re-
forms of the Second Vatican Council. It was also during his residency
in Mende that Durand finished his most ambitious liturgical work, the
Rationale divinorum officiorum,[9] or "Rationale for the Divine Offices."
The text, which actually began circulating in its first redaction as early
as 1291 or 1292, reached the final form of its second redaction c. 1294
to 1296.

The relative calm of Durand's life in his tiny diocese in Provence was
disrupted when the besieged Boniface VIII called him back to Rome
in the fall of 1295. He was immediately made rector (or papal ruler) of
the Anconian March and the Romagna, and entrusted with the difficult
task of raising an army to put down a rebellion by the antipapal Ghibel-
line faction, part of the ongoing saga of the papal-imperialist wars that
ravaged thirteenth-century Italy.[10] Durand's efforts ultimately ended in
failure, and by the spring of 1296, he resigned his office and took refuge
in the city of Rome, where he died on 1 November 1296. His final resting place was not in the soil of his native Provence but a tomb in the
Dominican basilica of Santa Maria sopra Minerva, where an effigy and
an epitaph honor his life and work.[11] Little could Durand have imagined
that within thirteen years of his death, the papacy and its administrative
apparatus would be moved to Provence, marking the beginning of the
much-maligned Avignon Papacy (1309–1378).

THE *RATIONALE* AND LITURGICAL COMMENTARY

Durand's capacious, encyclopedic allegorical exposition of the liturgical
rites of the Church is the best known medieval work in the genre of *Ex-*

positiones Missae, or "Mass expositions."[12] The nineteenth-century liturgist and founder of the monastery of Solesmes, Dom Prosper Guéranger, characterized the *Rationale* as a liturgical classic, declaring that it was the "final word" from the Middle Ages on the medieval Church's understanding of the liturgy.[13] Divided into eight books of varying length, the *Rationale* is exhaustive in its treatment of a wide variety of subjects: the church building and liturgical art, the ministers of the church and their functions, liturgical vestments, the Mass and the Divine Office, the Church's calendar, and its feast days.[14]

The genre that Durand synthesized and immortalized was nearly as ancient as Christianity itself. Dating back to the Patristic era, liturgical commentary continued to evolve throughout the Middle Ages into an elaborate and increasingly sophisticated literature. As the spatial setting and furnishings of the worship services of the medieval Latin Church became ever larger and more elaborate—with the quantum leap from Romanesque to Gothic art and architecture in the twelfth and thirteenth centuries—the genre of liturgical commentary followed suit.[15] Book 1 of the *Rationale*, with its lengthy and refined analysis of the windows, lattice work, pavement, choir, and vaulted ceilings of the Gothic cathedrals of Durand's epoch is a clear reflection of this change.[16] The themes and particular interpretations he offers have clear conceptual and textual antecedents in the great liturgists of the early Gothic Age of architecture—Honorius "of Autun" (c.1075/1080–1156),[17] (Ps.-)Hugh of St. Victor (c.1160–65),[18] and Sicardus of Cremona (c. 1150–1215).[19]

One thing that had not changed in the passage from the Romanesque to the Gothic Age of architecture was the method of liturgical exposition. Beginning with the Carolingian bishop Amalarius of Metz (c. 775/780–852/853),[20] liturgical commentary became an overwhelmingly allegorical tradition: every gesture, procession, vestment, and architectural structure could be scrutinized and interpreted allegorically as representing "higher" or "mystical" truths embodied in the performance of the liturgy. In his magisterial study of the development of the Roman Mass, Joseph Jungmann notes that Amalarius' enduring contribution to medieval liturgics was his codification of various forms of allegorical interpretation of the liturgy. Jungmann notes that Amalarius and his heirs most often employed "typological allegory" (fulfillments of Old Testament prophecies in Christ's ministry, life, and death) and "rememorative allegory" (linkage, remembrance, and reenactment of key events in Salvation history).[21] In the prologue of the *Rationale*, Durand himself provides a definition of allegory that is firmly rooted in this Amalarian tradition of liturgical exegesis:

Allegory is present when what is said literally has another meaning spiritually; for example, when one word or deed brings to mind another. If what is said is visible, then it is simply an allegory; if it is invisible and celestial, then it is called anagogy. Allegory also exists when an unrelated state of affairs is shown to exist through the use of strange or alien expressions; for example when the presence of Christ or the sacraments of the Church are signified in mystical words or signs; in words: *A branch shall come forth from the root of Jesse* [Isa 11:1], which plainly means: The Virgin Mary shall be born of the stock of David, who was the son of Jesse. Mystical deeds can signify in the same fashion the freedom of the people of Israel from Egyptian slavery by the blood of the [paschal] lamb, which signifies the Church snatched away from the clutches of the Devil through the Passion of Christ.[22]

As the critical apparatuses of the modern edition of the *Rationale* have clearly shown, Durand was much more of a "compiler" of his treatise than an "original" author in the modern sense. But this is precisely why the *Rationale* came to be viewed as the definitive treatment of the liturgy by his contemporaries and future generations of liturgists. Durand himself seems to attribute whatever success his treatise will have to his compilation method; at the end of his commentary he readily acknowledges his dependence upon previous expositors when he declares: "Like a honeybee, I have fruitfully gathered this [work] from diverse little booklets and the commentaries of others, as well as from the things which divine grace has furnished me."[23] The result of this "fruitful gathering" was the creation of a veritable summa of the allegorical tradition of liturgical exposition that began with Amalarius of Metz and culminated with Durand's skillful presentation of this tradition in his own exposition.

Book 1 of the *Rationale* vividly displays Durand's synthetic methods of compilation, even as he sometimes reworks his sources by expanding his commentary to reflect his mastery of canon law and Roman civil law.[24] In the first several chapters (1.1–1.4), and again in some of the later chapters (1.7–1.8), Durand follows a well established tradition of allegorically explicating the various parts of the church building, the altar, the pictures and ornaments with which churches are furnished, and the consecration or anointing of liturgical objects and ministers. Following the hermeneutical principles that he lucidly presents in the general prologue of the *Rationale*, Durand uncovers multiple layers of mystical signification in even the most mundane things: the pavement of the church building "is the foundation of our faith"(1.1.28); the beams, "which join the Lord's house, are the princes of the world or the preachers of the Church who defend the unity of the Church" (1.1.29); the roof tiles, "which repel rain from the Lord's house, are the soldiers who protect the church from pagans and other enemies" (1.1.36). In these chapters, Durand closely follows the presentation of his principal sources in both form and content: the allegorists Ps.-Hugh of St. Victor, Honorius of "Autun," and Sicardus of Cremona.

In his discussion of cemeteries (1.5), Durand temporarily abandons allegory. He closely follows the texts of his principal sources, the famous *Etymologies* of Isidore of Seville (c. 560–636)[25] and the liturgical *Summa* of the scholastic theologian John Beleth (d. 1182).[26] Durand presents an etymological and juridical discussion of the proper care of cemeteries and Christian mortuary practice. But his analysis can take some surprising turns, particularly when he brings his training as a canonist to bear on what were, in his day, "disputed questions." For example, he considers whether or not a woman who has died in childbirth can be given a funeral inside of the church building; the majority opinion among canonists is negative, but Durand himself argues that this "does not seem right." He argues in the affirmative, so long as no blood from her corpse "pollutes" the church.[27]

In his treatment of the rite for the consecration of a church (1.6), Durand returns to allegory, but he once again adds a plethora of juridical citations to his commentary. While working within the well-established allegorical tradition, Durand also mirrors the presentation of this rite found in his famous pontifical. Yet when he finished the second redaction of this chapter of book 1, he added fifteen new paragraphs (which constitute roughly half of this chapter in the second redaction) of material taken directly from canon law—principally Gratian's *Decretum* (c. 1140) and Greogry IX's *Liber Extra* (1234)—and Justinian's compilation of Roman civil law, the *Corpus Iuris Civilis* (529–534). In these new paragraphs Durand wrestles with myriad problems associated with the care of churches: for example, when or whether they should be reconsecrated if they have fallen into ruin or disrepair; who can claim sanctuary in a church, and under what conditions; and when a church can be considered desecrated and in need of "reconciliation" (that is, what sort of violence both inside or outside of the church building constitutes desecration).[28]

Book 1 closes with two chapters that, if read in the context of the other chapters, seem to be an appendage to the rest of this book. In fact, the title of book 1 found in the medieval manuscripts reveals as much when this distinction is made: "On the Church and Ecclesiastical Property and Furnishings; On Consecrations and the Sacraments." In his discussion in 1.8, Durand covers a wide range of consecrations, anointings, and blessings of individuals, liturgical vessels, and the implements with which these consecrations are done. While he invokes canon law texts in a number of instances, his interpretation is largely allegorical and is comparable to the material found in the early chapters of book 1.

The last chapter of the first book is somewhat puzzling. While it is titled "On the Sacraments," we soon discover that this little treatise is, in effect, a short manual on the sacrament of marriage that seems to have as its focus the many practical pastoral concerns of a parish priest who would administer this sacrament. This was a subject that Durand had already discussed at some length in the synodal statutes that he published for his diocesan clergy as bishop of Mende. The other sacraments are also extensively covered in other parts of the *Rationale*; the Eucharist, for example, receives almost an entire book (i.e., book 4, "On the Mass"). Durand may have well believed that marriage had to be discussed somewhere in his exposition, and book 1.9 may have seemed to be the only logical place in which to cover this subject.

THE NEW CRITICAL EDITION OF THE *RATIONALE*

Because of its capaciousness and Durand's editorial principle of synthesizing the entire medieval tradition of allegorical commentary, the *Rationale* superseded all previous liturgical commentaries within only a few years of its publication (c. 1292–1296). By the end of the fifteenth century, it had become one of the most widely disseminated treatises of its kind in Western Europe (and here I speak only of the medieval manuscripts, not the hundreds of printed editions that appeared in Europe in the early modern era). The *Rationale* is extant in over 200 medieval Latin manuscripts (including complete texts and substantial portions); it also survives in two well-known medieval vernacular translations (Middle French and Late Middle-High German). Moreover, Durand's commentary enjoyed the noteworthy distinction of being the second nonbiblical book to be printed at the Gutenberg press in Mainz, Germany (1459). From that point on it was reprinted 104 times (until 1859).[29]

Because of the voluminous manuscript tradition, the length of the work, and the complexity of its sources, no modern scholarly edition of the *Rationale* was ever published before the current edition was prepared by Fr. Anselme Davril, O.S.B., and myself. But this modern edition would have been impossible without the pioneering research of an

American scholar named Fr. Clarence Ménard, O.M.I., who completed a doctoral thesis on Durand at the Gregorian University in Rome (1967).[30] Fr. Ménard's unpublished thesis—which he generously provided to me in the summer of 1985 before we met in Boston—is the sine qua non of any modern research on the *Rationale*. Fr. Ménard spent a great many years traveling across Europe examining the majority of known medieval manuscripts of Durand's treatise and classified them into "families"; this analysis forms the bulk of his doctoral thesis. This work was done in anticipation of the production of a critical edition of the text that he was never able to undertake. But he generously encouraged us to continue his project, even as we corrected parts of his work and reclassified some of his manuscripts.

In May of 1990, as we sat within walking distance of the medieval cathedral of Mende, Fr. Davril and I discussed the basic contours of a proposed critical edition of Durand's lengthy commentary. With the expert advice, guidance, and enthusiastic support of Pierre-Marie Gy, O.P., Bertrand Guyot, O.P., and Mr. Luc Jocqué, Fr. Davril and I determined which medieval manuscripts we would employ as our best representatives for the two separate redactions of the *Rationale*[31] as we prepared the text for publication in the series *Corpus Christianorum, Continuatio Mediaeualis*. Another meeting with Fr. Davril and the above-named experts, this time within the peaceful confines of the Abbaye de Fleury in May of 1993, allowed us to resolve any lingering editorial concerns (particularly the construction of the various critical apparatuses that would accompany the Latin text).

In August of 1995, volume 1 of our edition was finally published (600 pp.). Fr. Davril and I then finished editorial work on the text of volume 2, which was published in May of 1998 (621 pp.). The third and final volume (468 pp.), published in 2000, contains the critical Latin text of books 7 and 8 of the *Rationale*; our complete analysis and commentary on the manuscripts; a study of the sources of text; and the complete indices for all three volumes of the work. The indices proved especially formidable since we had to identify and list all references to classical authors, canon law, biblical texts, patristic and medieval authors, and liturgical texts (hymns, antiphons, etc.).

PREVIOUS TRANSLATIONS:
MEDIEVAL AND MODERN

Not only did the *Rationale* enjoy immediate and lasting success in its Latin manuscript form, it also attracted the attention of medieval vernacular translators, who popularized portions of the text for a non-clerical audience. The earliest and perhaps best known of these transla-tions was the work of the French Carmelite Jean Golein (1325–1403). Working at the behest of the Valois king Charles V (r. 1364–1380), the founder of the library of the Palace of the Louvre, Golein produced a Middle French rendering of the fourth book of the *Rationale*, Durand's huge treatise on the Mass (c. 1372–1374).[32] Golein's translation was soon followed by others, including a Late Middle-High German translation of book 4 (c. 1384).[33]

Among the modern attempts to render Durand into a living lan-guage, pride of place must be given to that of the nineteenth-century Parisian author Charles Barthélemy.[34] In his general introduction, he laments the desecrations of the French Revolution while praising the virtues of the medieval allegorical mentality.[35] Barthélemy's staggering achievement—it remains the only complete vernacular translation of all eight books of the *Rationale*—numbers in the hundreds of pages. The breadth of this work is complemented by the beauty of the transla-tion, which features a fine balance between the literal sense of the text and an elegance of style characteristic of French romantic literature. I have come to view Barthélemy as a faithful companion in my own work on the *Rationale*. I have frequently compared my own translations to his work, often refining my prose in light of his rendering, sometimes questioning and rejecting his interpretation of particularly troublesome passages, but always inspired by the eloquence of his work. One of the serious drawbacks of his text, through no fault of Barthélemy himself, is the flawed Latin edition on which it was based (presumably a post-1600 printed edition of the *Rationale*).[36]

The only English translation of book 1 was published by the high-church Anglican cleric John Mason Neale (1818–1866). A prolific author and indefatigable student of medieval architecture, hymnody, and liturgy, Neale crusaded for the renovation and repair of the dilapidated Victo-rian churches of his day.[37] His Ecclesiological Society shared in common with the Tractarians of the Oxford Movement a desire to restore the spiritual majesty and aesthetic riches of medieval English Christendom (yet, unlike the famous Cardinal Newman, Neale remained faithful to Anglicanism). From his numerous works, we know how ardently Neale longed for a liturgical renaissance that would, as he believed, restore the dignity and reverence of Anglican worship, placing it firmly within the patristic and medieval Christian tradition of liturgical mystagogy.

Neale was an undisputed master of the poetic and stylistic nuances of ancient Greek and Latin hymnody, and his vernacular renditions of many classic hymns remain a much-beloved testimony to his many creative gifts. In 1843, Neale and his colleague Benjamin Webb published an English translation of the prologue and book 1 of the *Rationale*, a work that is suffused with the same literary charm and poetic sensibilities as his hymn translations.[38] Interestingly, his translation, which numbers 195 pages in the first edition, is preceded by a 132-page apologia for his devotion to the study of medieval symbolism. This tractate concludes with his joy at having found, in Durand, a brilliant proof-text with which to make his case for the revival of a mystagogical understanding of the liturgy:

> We have felt no small pleasure in thus enabling this excellent Prelate, though at so far distant a land from his own, and after silence of nearly six hundred years, being dead, yet to speak: and if the following pages are at all useful in pointing out the sacramental character of Catholick [*sic*] art, we shall be abundantly rewarded, as being fellow-workers with him in setting forth of one, now too much forgotten, Church principle.[39]

Yet, despite the elegance of its elaborate Victorian rhetorical structures, the Neale translation is too antiquated for the modern English-speaking student of medieval liturgy and architecture. Indeed, the difficulty of Neale's now obsolete prose is by itself a compelling argument for a modern English translation. But there are other more serious problems with his translation. To start with, he had to employ the faulty Latin texts that were available to him: an early edition from Rome (1473) and the Venetian edition of 1599, which is actually a reprint edition of the famous, though flawed, Nicholas Doard edition from Lyons (1551). These Latin editions also lack any sort of critical apparatus or apparatus of sources. Neale also chose not to translate many passages from Durand's text that he perhaps judged as being too salacious; for example, Durand's discussion of the consummation of a marriage in 1.9.8 and 1.9.11 (in the former passage he omits an entire paragraph, in the latter his translation of that paragraph ends with an ellipsis).[40] In fairness to Neale, it should be noted that Barthélemy also leaves untranslated many such passages, but unlike Neale, he includes those texts in the original Latin.

RULES FOR THE NEW ENGLISH TRANSLATION

My own translation of the general prologue and book 1 is based on the critical Latin text that Fr. Davril and I published in the first volume of our edition. For an exhaustive treatment of the manuscript tradition of the medieval text, as well as the specific manuscripts that were employed for the edition, the reader should consult the last volume of our three-volume work. It contains all of our introductory material, including my own source analysis and the indices for the complete work (prologue and books 1 through 8). No other translation to date has been based on a critical text of this sort.

I trust that my long familiarity with the construction of the Latin text (based on more than a decade of editorial work) has given me some advantage when I set myself to the task of translating Durand's liturgical magnum opus. Nonetheless, I have had to wrestle with a number of problems associated with the attempt to make the rhetorical structure and nuances of one language clear in another. My chief aim in this regard has been to balance fidelity to the literal meaning against readability for a modern audience; the worst that can be said of a translation is that "it reads like a translation." More often than not, where Durand's scholastic grammar is particularly vexing or defies easy translation into modern American English, I have striven for readability and faithfulness to the spirit rather than the letter of what he said.

When read straight through, however, the present translation may sometimes strike the reader as uneven or rhetorically inconsistent. But Durand's *Rationale* was itself based on a wide range of sources, most of which he copied verbatim. Unlike, for example, the works of St. Gregory the Great or St. Bernard of Clairvaux, Durand's treatise was by design an encyclopedic compendium of a remarkable variety of texts, from radically different genres (often composed centuries apart). Some passages are astonishingly poetic—when, for example, Durand clearly follows the allegorical liturgical explications of his predecessors. Some portions are matter-of-fact, or even pedantic—as when he cites the rubrics and texts of liturgical books used for various rites (for example, when he follows his own pontifical). Other portions are turgid, mentally taxing, and often difficult for a modern reader to follow—as when he cites a plethora of legal texts from Roman civil law or medieval canon law. Particularly noteworthy is his discussion in 1.6 on the rite for the consecration of a church; roughly half of this chapter consists of paraphrases or citations of these legal sources. I have tried, as much as possible, to remain faithful to the rhetorical structure of these disparate sources while providing, to the best of my ability, a consistent, flowing text.

There are numerous citations from Scripture throughout the *Rationale*. Most of these are derived from Jerome's Vulgate translation (or, I should say, the Vulgate as it was used in the liturgical and legal texts of the Church). I have resisted the practice of some modern translators of patristic and medieval authors of presenting these passages in the official English version of some modern Bible. Many of Durand's references to the Bible come from the liturgy or from collections of medieval canon law, where the text is slightly (or sometimes startlingly) different from modern critical editions of the Vulgate, not to mention the critical editions of the Hebrew Scriptures or the Greek New Testament upon which modern English translations are based. The biblical references provided in brackets are collated to the Latin Vulgate version of the Bible (and sometimes have different verse numbers than modern English translations based on the original languages).[41]

Many times Durand presents a biblical passage as if it were a literal passage, when in fact it is a paraphrase. This posed problems in the critical edition of the *Rationale*; we settled on the rule of italicizing such texts since Durand himself presented them as citations, even though they were inaccurate. In other cases, where he is clearly making an allusion or a very loose paraphrase, we kept the text in standard font, with a reference (cf.) in the apparatus of sources. In the present translation, I have provided both types of reference in brackets within the body of the text (literal citations, paraphrases, and allusions).

There are many instances where Durand provides elaborate and sometimes fanciful etymologies of key terms, often following the lead of the famed medieval etymologist, Isidore of Seville; the nuances and puns of these texts are invariably lost in translation. In such cases I have attempted to communicate the nuance by including the Latin term(s) in brackets so that the reader has some sense of the word play in the original text.

A final word about the presentation of sources used by Durand. The Latin edition of the *Rationale* features a running source apparatus where I have identified every direct or probable source used by the bishop of Mende in the composition of his text (direct quotations, paraphrases, or textual parallels). In the present translation, I have only included notes with complete bibliographic citation when Durand himself identifies or directly cites a particular source within the body of his commentary.

THE RATIONALE DIVINORUM OFFICIORUM
OF WILLIAM DURAND OF MENDE

{ Prologue }

ON THE CHURCH BUILDING AND ECCLESIASTICAL
PROPERTY AND FURNISHINGS;
ON CONSECRATIONS AND THE SACRAMENTS

1. Whatever belongs to the liturgical offices, objects, and furnishings of the Church is full of signs of the divine and the sacred mysteries, and each of them overflows with a celestial sweetness when it is encountered by a diligent observer who can extract *honey from rock and oil from the stoniest ground* [Deut 32:13]. Who knows *the order of the heavens and can apply its rules to the earth* [Job 38:33]? Certainly, he who would attempt to investigate the majesty of heaven would be overwhelmed by its glory. It is, in fact, a deep well from which I cannot drink [cf. Jn 4:11], unless He who *gives all things abundantly and does not reproach us* [Jas 1:5] provides me with a vessel *so that I can drink with joy from the fountains of the Savior* [Isa 12:3] *which flow between the mountains* [Ps 103:10].

A reason cannot always be given for everything that has been handed down to us by our predecessors;[1] and because that which lacks an explanation must be uprooted, I, William, bishop of the holy church of Mende, by the indulgence of God alone, knocking at the door, will continue to knock, until the key of David deigns to open it for me [cf. Rev 3:20], so that the *king might bring me into his cellar where he stores his wine* [Song 2:4]. Here the celestial model that was shown to Moses on the mountaintop will be revealed to me [cf. Ex 20], so that I can unveil and explain clearly and openly each object or ornament[2] that belongs to the ecclesiastical services, what each of these signifies or represents figuratively, and set forth their rationale, according to that which has been revealed by Him *who makes the tongues of infants speak eloquently* [Wis 10:21], *whose Spirit blows where it wishes* [Jn 3:8], *and gives to each one as it deserves* [1 Cor 12:11], to the praise and glory of the Trinity.

2. We rightly receive the sacraments as signs or figures, since figures are not themselves the virtues but signs of the virtues, just as men are instructed through use of writing. Moreover, some signs are natural while others are posited by men; this topic, along with what a sacrament is, will be discussed in the fourth part, concerning the seventh portion of the Canon of the Mass, under the words, "Mystery of Faith."[3]

3. The priests and prelates of the Church, to whom it has been given to know these mysteries, as Luke testifies [cf. Lk 8:10], who are the bearers and dispensers of the sacraments, must understand these sacraments and shine with the virtues that they represent so that through their light, others may similarly be illumined. Otherwise, they are the blind leading the blind [cf. Mt 14:14], as the Prophet testifies: *Their eyes have been blinded so they cannot see* [Ps 68:24]. But, it is sad to say, nowadays most of those priests who manage the Church's affairs and conduct its worship on a day-to-day basis have little or no understanding of what the Divine Offices[4] signify or why they were instituted, and in fact, the words of the Prophet Isaiah appear to be fulfilled literally: *The priest and layman are alike* [Isa 24:2]. For in presenting the sacred loaves at the table of the Lord, they neither see nor understand these mysteries; God will undoubtedly judge them justly as though they were mere beasts of burden carrying bread for others. For this ignorance they shall be held accountable on the day of wrath and judgment; when the cedars of Paradise tremble, what shall the desert shrub do? They were addressed by the Prophet, where he says: *They have not known my ways, whom in my anger I judge, if they enter into my rest* [Ps 94:11, Vulg.].[5]

4. Now the professors of the liberal and any other arts commonly struggle to adorn, support, and color with reasons and causes any of the simple, circumstantial, or unexplained matters contained within their arts. Painters and artisans, in whatever mechanical arts, or builders, in whatever work they undertake, strive to provide or have at hand probable reasons and causes. And according to the earthly laws by which men live, it is shameful for a nobleman engaged in his business to be ignorant of the very law in which he is versed.[6]

5. And while learning is especially necessary for priests to understand doctrine, simple priests should not be disparaged by the learned, as it is written: *You shall not disparage God* [Ex 22:28].[7] Thus, according to Augustine: "The learned should not laugh, if by chance they hear certain bishops and ministers of the Church invoke God with barbarisms or grammatical errors, or if they do not understand the meaning of the words they pronounce, or if they can only distinguish the words confus-

ingly; not that such things do not need correction, but, because they are done piously, they should be tolerated."[8] What priests should know is discussed in the second part, in the treatise, *On priests.*[9]

6. While it does not seem that those things that are done in the ecclesiastical rites and offices are done figuratively—because figures have diminished in importance, and today is the age of the Truth, and we should not Judaize[10]—those figures, which have diminished in importance, when today the Truth has appeared, still, in fact, conceal a multiplicity of truths that we cannot see, on account of which the Church still uses figures. For example, in white vestments we understand in a certain sense the beauty of our souls, namely the glory of our immortality, which we cannot plainly see; and in the Mass, the events leading to the Passion of Christ are represented in the Preface,[11] so that those things will be held more firmly and more faithfully in our memory.

7. It should also be noted that among those things contained in the Law, some are moral and some are mystical.[12] Those which are moral shape our character, and must be understood in the sense of the very words they speak, such as: *Love God, honor your father, you shall not kill* [Deut 6:5, 5:16–17], and other things of this sort. Mystical figures are those that signify something else beyond their literal meaning. Among these, some are sacramental while others are ceremonial. Those things are called sacramental for which a clear reason can be given why they were decreed in the Law, such as circumcision, the observance of the Sabbath, and things of this sort. Those things are called ceremonial, for which no clear reason can be given why they were decreed in the Law, such as: *You shall not plow with an ox and an ass, you shall not wear a garment made of wool and cloth, you shall not plant a field with different seeds* [Deut 22:10–11; Lev 19:19], and things of this sort.

8. The Law, then, as it pertains to morals has not undergone mutation, but as it pertains to sacramental and ceremonial things it has changed, but only on an outward level; the mystical understanding of these things has not changed, and so it cannot be said that the Law has changed as much as it has been passed on to us, just as the priesthood has been transferred to us.[13]

9. It must be noted that in Holy Scripture there is a historical, allegorical, tropological, and anagogical sense, and so according to Boethius: "All divine authority is understood either historically or allegorically, or from a combination of both senses."[14] And according to Jerome,[15] we must scrutinize sacred Scripture for its moral character: first, according to its literal sense; second, allegorically, that is, for its spiritual

understanding; third, according to its prefigurement of future blessedness. History is when the words describe an actual event, when for example, whatever is being said is described entirely as it occurred; for example, when it is written that the people of Israel built a tabernacle for
the Lord when they were saved from Egypt. And the term history comes
from *ystorin*, which means, "to make gestures;" hence it is as if those
who are called stage actors [*ystriones*] were historical narrators.[16]

10. Allegory is present when what is said literally has another meaning spiritually; for example, when one word or deed brings to mind another. If what is represented is visible, then it is simply an allegory; if it
is invisible and celestial, then it is called anagogy.[17] Allegory also exists
when an unrelated state of affairs is shown to exist through the use of
strange or alien expressions; when, for example, the presence of Christ
or the sacraments of the Church are signified in mystical words or signs;
in words: *A branch shall come forth from the root of Jesse* [Isa 11:1], which
plainly means: the Virgin Mary shall be born of the stock of David, who
was the son of Jesse. Mystical deeds can signify in the same fashion the
freedom of the people of Israel from Egyptian slavery by the blood of
[paschal] lamb, which signifies the Church snatched away from the
clutches of the Devil through the Passion of Christ. The word allegory
comes from the Greek word, *aleon*, which means "strange" and *gore*,
which is "sense;" that is, allegory means having "another sense."[18]

11. Tropology is the correction of manners or moral speech for the
correction and foundation of morals, presented either mystically or
plainly; mystically, where it says: *At all times let your garments be white,
and spare not the oil from your head* [Eccl 9:8], that is, may your works
be pure, and may charity never fall away from your intentions. And
then, "It is necessary that David kills the Goliath in us," that is, that humility overcome pride. And then plainly, where it says: *Share your bread
with the hungry* [Is 58:7], and here: *Let us not love with our tongue or in
word, but in deed and truth* [1 Jn 3:18]. Tropology comes from the word
tropos, that is "conversion," and *logos*, that is "speech," as if to say "speech
that converts."

12. Anagogy comes from *ana*, which is "upward," and *goge*, which is
"lead, "as if to say, "lead upward." Hence that which is called the anagogical sense leads us from visible to invisible things, as the light that was
created on the first day signifies something invisible, that is, the angelic
nature created in the beginning of time. Anagogy is therefore a sense of
speech that leads to higher things or things above the heavens, namely,
the Trinity and the orders of angels, or the future reward and future life

in heaven, discussed plainly or in mystical words. Plainly, where it says: *Blessed are the pure of heart for they shall see God* [Mt 5:8]; and mystically, where it says: *Blessed are they who wash their robes, that they may have the right to the tree of life and that they may enter the city through the gates* [Rev 22:14], which plainly means: Blessed is he who purifies his thoughts, that to him shall be given the right to see God, who is the way, the truth and the life [cf. Jn 14:6]; and through doctrine, that is the example of the Fathers, he shall enter into the reign of God. Similarly, Jerusalem is understood historically as that earthly city that pilgrims seek; allegorically, it represents the church militant; tropologically, any faithful soul; anagogically, the heavenly Jerusalem, or our homeland. Other examples on this subject can be seen in the lessons, which are read on Holy Saturday, as discussed in the sixth part of this treatise.[19] Often in this work different senses of interpretation are employed for the same thing, passing from one sense to another, and the diligent reader shall be able to observe how this happens. Just as no one is prohibited from employing diverse exceptions or defenses in legal proceedings,[20] neither should anyone be barred from using a variety of explanations in the praise of God, with the faith always being preserved.

13. It is necessary to consider that numerous variations in rites can be discovered in the divine liturgy. Indeed, each church has, for the most part, its own observances, which in their own sense abound, but it should not be judged reprehensible or absurd to venerate God or his saints with a variety of songs, melodies, and observances, since according to the Prophet, the Church triumphant is clothed with diverse attire [cf. Ps 44:10]; and in the administration of the ecclesiastical sacraments a variety of customs is tolerated by law. And so according to Augustine: "We have received some of the ecclesiastical institutions in the Divine Office from Holy Scripture, some from apostolic tradition without the authority of Scripture, confirmed by the apostles' successors, and some, whose origins are unknown, are confirmed by custom and approved by practice, to which equal observance is owed as to other rites."[21]

14. The reader should not be disturbed if he reads about things in this work that he finds are not observed in his own church, or if he does not find something that is observed there. For we shall not proceed to discuss the peculiar observances of any particular place but the rites that are more common and more ordinary, since we have labored to set forth a universal teaching and not one of particular bearing; nor would it be possible for us to examine thoroughly the peculiar observances of all places. We have therefore resolved, for the salvation of our soul and the

benefit of the reader, to explain as clearly as possible the secret mysteries of the Divine Offices and then to arrange and explain thoroughly
those things that seemed necessary for understanding the daily services
for clerics, just as we are known to have done faithfully in our *Judicial
Mirror*, for those employed in the secular courts, whose status is entirely
different [from clerics].[22]

15. Nevertheless, it must be carefully considered that concerning
these Divine Offices, there are many ordinary observances whose institution can be given neither a moral nor mystical explanation; but some
are recognized out of necessity, some on account of their suitability,
others on account of the difference between the Old and New Law, others on account of their appropriateness, others on account of the grand
celebration and reverence for those offices that are long since fixed.
Thus, according to Saint Augustine: "There is such an innumerable diversity of practices in so many places that we could scarcely if ever discover the causes which led men to establish the rules they follow."[23]

16. The word *Rationale* is appropriately used as the title of this book,
because just as "revelation and truth" were written on the pectoral of
judgment that the High Priest bore on his vestments,[24] so too the *Rationale* contains the reasons for the variations in the Divine Offices, and
their inner meaning is described and made manifest. The prelates and
priests of the Church should faithfully keep these truths in the chamber
of their heart. In the pectoral of judgment, moreover, there was a stone
by whose splendor the sons of Israel could know that God's favor was
with them. In the same way, the devout reader, instructed in the mysteries of the divine offices by the splendor of this book, will be able to know
that God's favor will be with us, unless we incur his indignation through
the commission of some sin. The pectoral was embroidered with four
colors and golden thread, and now, as I stated before, the reasons for the
variety of ecclesiastical offices can be said to correspond to these four
colors and are understood through the four senses: namely, the historical, allegorical, tropological, and anagogical, with faith [gold] at the cen-
ter of all colors.

17. This book is divided into eight parts, through which we shall proceed one by one, the Lord willing. In the first part, the church building,
ecclesiastical property and furnishings, consecrations, and the sacraments are treated; in the second, the ministers of the Church and their
duties; in the third, the priestly vestments and other garments; in the
fourth, the Mass and the things performed in each of its parts; in the

fifth, the other ecclesiastical offices in general; in the sixth, on the special offices of Sundays, holy days, and feast days associated with the Lord; in the seventh, the feasts of Saints, the Office for the Dedication of a Church, and the Office of the Dead; in the eighth, on the *computus* and the calendar.

BOOK ONE

◈ ON THE CHURCH BUILDING ◈
AND ECCLESIASTICAL PROPERTY
AND FURNISHINGS; ON CONSECRATIONS
AND THE SACRAMENTS

[1]

ON THE CHURCH BUILDING AND ITS PARTS

In the first part of this work we have decided to treat certain topics in general, namely: the church[1] and its parts; the altar; pictures, images, and ecclesiastical ornaments; bells; the cemetery, and other sacred and religious places; the consecration of a church; the consecration of an altar; consecrations and anointings; the ecclesiastical sacraments.

1. The first thing we shall consider is the church building and its parts. It should be noted that concerning churchly things, some items pertain to the physical structure in which the divine offices are celebrated; others are spiritual, that is, they apply to the community of the faithful, or the people who have been gathered as one by their ministers, by Him who makes them dwell in one accord in his house [cf. Ps 67:7]. Just as the physical building is constructed from a group of stones joined together, so too the Church is spiritually constructed of diverse men gathered together.

2. Church, which is a Greek word, means "convocation" in Latin, because the Church calls everyone to herself; and this name corresponds more appropriately to the spiritual definition of the Church than the material because here, men are gathered together, not stones; though oftentimes, the name of the thing signified is attributed to the thing that it signifies. The material Church thus represents the spiritual, as noted where the consecration of a church is discussed.[2] On the other hand, the Church is called "catholic" in Greek, that is, universal, because it is established and extended throughout the world, because those who believe in God throughout the world should be gathered in one congregation, or because in her subsists a universal doctrine for the instruction of all the faithful.

3. Synagogue means "congregation" in Greek, which is a name that was used by the Jewish people itself.[3] It was customary to still call their gathering a synagogue even when the term church was being used; however, the Apostles never used the term synagogue but always church, perhaps to make a distinction between the two.

4. The present Church is called Zion on account of its pilgrimage on earth; though far removed from the promise of its celestial blessings, the Church contemplates them; therefore Zion means "contemplation."[4] And on account of its future homeland and its peace, it is called Jerusalem, a name that means "vision of peace."[5] The Church is also called the house of God, which is derived from the word *dogma*, which in Greek means "morally upright," as if to say in God's house, men are especially in one accord. Sometimes we say *kyriaca*, that is Lord's house; sometimes *basilica*, which is Greek and in Latin means, a "king's residence," or "regal" place [*regalis*] from king [*rex*], that is, from the word for king [*basilio*] in Greek; the earthly palaces of kings are so named, but our house of prayer is called a king's residence because the King of Kings is served there. Sometimes the Church is called a temple, as if to say that it is a huge canopy [*tectum amplum*] under which sacrifices are offered to God our King; sometimes it is called God's tabernacle, since this life on earth is a pilgrimage, and in this journey the Church proceeds to the fatherland, as we now say; or sometimes it is called a tabernacle as if to say it is "God's inn" [*taberna Dei*], as is noted in the sixth part, *On the dedication of a church*.[6] Why the Church is also called the Tabernacle or Ark of the Covenant will be discussed in the part *On the altar*.[7] Sometimes a Church is called a *martyrium*, since it exists in honor of some martyr; sometimes it is called a chapel, for the reason noted in the second part, in the treatise *On the priesthood*;[8] sometimes it is called a cloister; sometimes a sacristy; sometimes a sanctuary; sometimes a house of prayer; sometimes a monastery; and sometimes an oratory. Nevertheless, generally speaking, any place established for prayer can be called an oratory.

Moreover, the Church is sometimes called the Body of Christ; sometimes it is called a virgin, according to the text: *The jealousy I feel for you*, etc. [2 Cor 11:2]. Sometimes it is called a bride to whom Christ has betrothed himself in faith, about which we read in the Gospel: *He who has the bride is the bridegroom* [Jn 3:29]. Sometimes it is called a mother because she daily provides God with spiritual sons through Baptism; sometimes, she is called a daughter, according to the Prophet: *In place of your fathers, daughters are born to you* [Ps 44:17]. Also, the Church is regarded as a widow, because on account of her afflictions, she grows dark, just as Rachel could not be consoled [cf. Jer 31:15]. Sometimes she is depicted as a harlot because she is assembled from among the nations, and because she closes her bosom to no one returning to her. Sometimes she is called a city—on account of the communion of her saints, her citizens—walled with the fortification of the Scriptures, by which heretics are beaten back; she has diverse types of stones and tongues because the merits of each of her members are diverse, as we shall see. Whatever the synagogue received from the Law, the Church now receives through grace from Christ, who is her bridegroom, replacing it with something better. To be sure, the foundation of an oratory or church is nothing new. For example, the Lord decreed to Moses on Mount Sinai that he make a Tabernacle with wonderfully fashioned curtains; it was divided into two parts by a veil, whose first part was called "holy" where the people offered sacrifice; the interior was called the "Holy of Holies," where the priests and Levites ministered [cf. Ex 26:31–37], as noted the prologue of the fourth part.[9]

5. And after this Tabernacle was consumed by old age, the Lord commanded that a Temple be built that Solomon constructed, in a most marvelous manner, which was divided into two parts just as the Tabernacle was [1 Chr 8:1–66]. From both—that is, from the Tabernacle and the Temple—our material church takes its form, in whose outer part, the people listen and pray; in the sanctuary the clergy pray, preach, offer praises, and minister.

6. Moreover, the Tabernacle, because it was made during the wandering of the Israelites, sometimes serves as a figure of the world, which passes away, and its concupiscence; and for that reason it consists of the four colors of the curtains, just as the world was composed of four elements. Therefore God in the Tabernacle is God in this world. Just as the Temple was reddened with the blood of Christ, the Tabernacle clearly serves as figure of the Church militant, which does not have a permanent earthly city but seeks a future one [cf. Heb 13:14]; therefore, it is called a "tent [*tabernaculum*]," for tents are the dwellings of soldiers. God in the Tabernacle is God among the faithful who are gathered together in his name. The first part of the Temple, in which the people used to sacrifice, is the active life, in which the people labored in the love of their neighbors; the other part, in which the Levites ministered, is the contemplative life in which the love and contemplation of God is the

only task for a pure gathering of religious men. The Tabernacle is transformed into a Temple because one hastens from warfare to a triumph.[10]

7. A church must therefore be built as follows: after having prepared the place of its foundation, according to the text "The Lord's house is well established on a solid rock,"[11] the bishop or priest who has permission to preside, sprinkles it with holy water to banish thenceforth the demonic spirits, and places the principal stone, into which a cross is imprinted, on the foundation.[12]

8. A church should also be built as follows: that its head properly look towards the east—about which we shall speak in the prologue of the fifth part[13]—namely, towards the rising point of the equinoctial sun, thus signifying that the Church, while battling in this world, should display moderation and equanimity, in both prosperity and adversity; it should not therefore face the rising point of the midsummer sun, as some do. Besides, if the walls of Jerusalem were built into a city by the Jews, at the order of the Lord, as the Prophet says [cf. Ps 121:3], how much more should we build up the walls of our churches.

9. Indeed, the material church in which the people have come to praise God signifies the holy Church in heaven, constructed of living stones. This is the Lord's house, firmly built, whose foundation is Christ, the cornerstone; the foundation upon whom have been placed the Apostles and Prophets [cf. Eph 2:20], just as it is written: *His foundations on the holy mountains* [Ps 86:1]. Those built-up walls are the Jews and the Gentiles, coming to Christ from the four corners of the world, who have believed, continue to believe, and will believe in Him. Moreover, those faithful who are predestined for life are the stones in this structure whose walls will continue to be built until the end of this world. Stone is placed on top of stone when the teachers of the Church attend to the education of her children, for their teaching, correction, and fortification in the holy Church. He who takes upon himself the burden of his brother carries a stone, so to speak, for the construction of the Church. The bigger stones, and the polished or square ones that are placed on the outside wall—in the middle of which lie the smaller ones—are the more perfected men whose merits and prayers sustain the weaker men in the holy Church.

10. Moreover, the cement, without which the wall cannot remain steadfast, is made of lime, sand and water. The lime is fervent charity which joins itself to the sand, that is, earthly works, because true charity

contains the greatest concern for others, joined with care for widows, the elderly, orphans, and the infirm; therefore, those who have charity desire ardently to work with their hands that those hands might help others. In order that the lime and the earth can be used to build the wall, they are bound together with a mixture of water. Since the water represents the Holy Spirit—just as the stones cannot be joined to build a stable wall without cement—so too neither can men be joined together to build the Heavenly Jerusalem without charity, through which the Holy Spirit conducts their work. All of the stones in the wall are polished, squared, fine, and firm, that is, they represent the Saints; namely, those are arranged by the hands of the Supreme Artisan to remain constant in the Church, among whom some are carried by others, while they bear no burdens, such as the more simple members of the Church; others are supported while they bear others, such as those in the middle [the clergy]; and others carry burdens but are not borne by others—unless they are supported by Christ, who is their sole foundation—such as the perfected. One charity joins all of them in the manner of cement, so to speak, as long as the living stones are joined together in peace. Christ was our wall in His discourse, and our rampart in His Passion.

11. Certainly, when the Jews were building the walls of Jerusalem, their enemies ranged against them to impede their work, to such an extent, that as we read in Ezra [cf. Ezra 4:7], when attacked by their enemies, they were laying stones in the wall with one hand, and with another hand they were fighting against them. And we too, building the walls of the Church, are surrounded by enemies, namely our vices, or perverse men who wish to impede our works. Thus when building up the walls, that is the virtues, we attack the enemy; and according to the custom of the Jewish people, we bear our weapons, that is: *The shield of faith, the breastplate of justice, the helmet of salvation, the sword of God's word* [Eph 6:14–17], in our hands so that we can defend ourselves against them, and our pastor or priest represents Christ for us, who teaches us in the readings and protects us in his prayers.

12. Next, in the Old Testament, the Lord showed out of what material the Tabernacle should be made, saying to Moses in Exodus 25 and 35: Collect the *first fruits*, that is, whatever is precious among the people of Israel, but receive them only from him who shall offer it on his own accord, namely: gold, *silver and bronze; hyacinth, purple and twice-dyed scarlet, that is, goat's hair; and hyacinth, purple and scarlet-colored linen*, that is a type of fabric from Egypt which is supple and white; *and*

goat's hairs and ram's skins dyed red, which we call "Parthian," since the Parthians were the first to have thought to dye them in this manner; and hyacinth-colored skins and *shittim* wood [Ex 25:2–5; cf. Ex 30:1–6].[14]

13. And *Shittim* is the name of a mountain, a region, and a tree that is similar to a white thorn bush in its flowers; and it is a light wood, incorruptible and unconsumed by fire. And oil for the lamps, spices for the perfumes and sweet-smelling incense; onyx and other precious stones and gems with which they shall make a sanctuary for me, in which I shall dwell in their midst, lest they have to worry about returning to the mountain [cf. Ex 35:8–9]. These things, fully covered by the Master in his *Histories*, can be followed in his commentary on Exodus.[15]

14. The arrangement of the materials of the church can be likened to the human body. The chancel, that is the place where the altar is, represents the head; the cross, from either side, represents the arms or the hands,[16] while the remaining part extending to the west is seen as the rest of the body. The sacrifice of the altar signifies the offerings of the heart, and according to Richard of St. Victor,[17] the arrangement of the church signifies the threefold ordering of those saved in the Church: the sanctuary signifies the order of virgins; the choir, the order of the continent; the body of the church, the married. The sanctuary is narrower than the choir and the choir is narrower than the body because there are fewer virgins than continent, and fewer still of them than there are married. Therefore, the sanctuary is a more sacred place than the choir, and the choir more sacred than the body, because the order of virgins is nobler than the order of the continent, and their order is nobler than the married.

15. Now the church, with its four walls, that is, the doctrine of the four Gospels, rises far and wide towards the heights, that is, in the heights of virtue; its length is its long suffering, which patiently tolerates adversity until it arrives at its celestial homeland; its width is its charity, which broadens the soul of man to love his friends in God and to love his enemies on behalf of God; the height [of the nave] is the hope of the future redemption, which makes man despise prosperity and adversity until he shall see the blessings of the Lord in the land of the living.

16. Again, the foundation of the temple of God or His grace is faith in things not seen; the roof is charity, which covers a multitude of sins [cf. 1 Pet 4:8]; the door is obedience, about which the Lord said: *If you wish to enter into eternal life, obey the commandments* [Mt 19:17]; the pavement is humility, about which the Psalmists says: *My soul clings to the pavement* [Ps 118:25].

17. The four outer walls of the church are the four cardinal virtues: justice, fortitude, prudence, and temperance; in the Book of Apocalypse these are the four outer walls, of equal size, of the heavenly city. The windows are hospitality with cheerfulness and mercy with kindness, about which the Lord said: *We will come to Him and we will make our home with Him* [Jn 14:23]. Still, some churches are built in the form of a cross to show that we should crucify ourselves to the world, or that we should follow the way of the cross, according to what is written: *He who wishes to follow me must deny himself and carry his cross and follow me* [Mt 16:24]. Yet some churches are formed in the shape of round circles, which signifies that the Church extends itself to encompass the whole world, for which reason it is said: *And to the ends of the world their words* [Ps 18:5], or from the circle of the world, we will come to the circle of the crown of eternity.

18. The choir of the clergy is the harmonious gathering place of the singers, or the multitude gathered for the sacred mysteries.[18] The word chorus comes from "circular dance [*chorea*]" or "crown [*corona*]." For in the past, clerics used to stand in a circle around the altar, and they used to sing psalms in unison, but Flavianus and Theodorus instituted antiphonal psalmody, instructed by Ignatius, who himself received divine instruction on this matter.[19] The two choirs of singers represent the angels and the spirits of the just, as if to say in singing praises back and forth, they exhort each other to do good works. Others say that chorus comes from the word "concord [*concordia*]," which exists with charity, because he who lacks charity cannot sing in unison with others. What this chorus signifies, and why the older members are seated last, will be discussed in the fourth part, under the heading *On the Introit*,[20] and also under the heading, *On the accession of the pontiff to the altar*.[21] And note that when one person sings it is called "monody [*monodia*]" in Greek, *cicinium* in Latin; and when two sing it is called *bicinium*; when many sing it is called a "chorus."[22]

19. The hallway [*exedra*] is arched or vaulted and sometimes a bit separated from the temple or palace, from which it gets its name because it sticks outside [*extra heret*] of the wall; in Greek it is called *sydon* and it signifies the faithful laity clinging to Christ and the Church. The crypts or underground grottoes that they make in some churches represent the hermits, inasmuch as they are cultivators of a more private life.

20. The atrium of the church signifies Christ, through whom the entrance to the celestial Jerusalem is opened, which is called a porch

[*porticus*], and is thus named from the word "gate [*porta*]," that it might be opened wide [*aperta*].

21. The towers of the church are the preachers and prelates of the Church who are its fortification and defense; thus the groom speaks to his bride in the canticle of love: *Your neck is like David's tower, built up with bulwarks* [Song 4:4]. The pinnacle of the tower represents the life or mind of the prelate that directs itself to higher things.

22. The rooster placed on the top of the church signifies the preachers; in the dead of night, the ever watchful rooster divides the hours with his crowing, arouses those sleeping, and announces the approaching day; but first he arouses himself to crow by flapping his wings. Each of these things is not lacking in sacred mystery: night is this world; those sleeping are the sons of night lying in sin; the rooster represents the preachers who preach clearly and awaken the sleeping so that they might cast away the works of darkness, crying out: Woe to those sleeping, *arise you who sleep*[23] [Eph 5:14], announcing the future light, when they preach the day of judgment and future glory. And prudently, before preaching the virtues to others, they awaken themselves from the sleep of sin, chastising their bodies, which is why the Apostle says: *I chastise my body*, etc. [1 Cor 9:27]. Just as the rooster on the spire does, the preachers also turn themselves against the wind when rebuking or arguing against the rebels, vigorously resisting them, lest when the wolf comes they are accused of having fled. The iron rod upon which the rooster sits represents the correct teaching of the preacher,[24] and that he must not speak from the spirit of man but of God, according to which it says: *If anyone speaks, let it be as if it were the teachings of God*, etc. [1 Pet 4:11]. And, that this rod is on top of the cross or placed on the summit point of the church, implies that the words of Scripture are consummated or confirmed, for which reason the Lord said in His Passion, *It is finished* [Jn 19:30], and His title was indelibly written above Him.[25]

23. The dome, that is, the lofty and rotund summit of the temple upon which a cross is placed, on account of its roundness, signifies how the perfect and inviolable Catholic faith must be preached and maintained, and how unless anyone preserves that faith completely and inviolably, he shall perish through all eternity.

24. The glass windows of the church are the divine Scriptures that repel the wind and rain, that is, they prevent harmful things from entering; and when they transmit the brightness of the true sun (that is, God) into the church (that is, the hearts of the faithful), they illumine those dwelling there. These windows are larger on the inside of the church be-

cause the mystical sense is broader and surpasses the literal sense. The five corporeal senses are also signified by the windows, which must be well structured on the outside, lest they allow in the vanities of the world; and they are open within to acquire more freely the spiritual gifts.

25. We take the lattice work that is in front of the windows to be the Prophets or other obscure teachers of the Church militant, in whom we understand the two precepts of charity whenever two columns are placed side by side, by reason of the fact that the Apostles were sent out two by two to preach [cf. Lk 10:1].

26. The door of the church is Christ; thus in the Gospel the Lord said: *I am the doorway* [Jn 10:9]. The Apostles are also doorways of the Church. The word doorway [*ostium*] comes from *obsistendo*, "standing in front of those outdoors;" or from *ostendendo*, "showing the entry way." The leaf of a door [*valva*] comes from *volvendo*, "turning or opening;" door [*porta*] comes from *portando*, "carrying," since whatever is brought in is carried through the doorway.[26]

27. The columns of the church are the bishops or teachers who spiritually hold up the temple of God, just as the Evangelists hold up the throne of God. This is why they are called, on account of the melodiousness of their divine eloquence, silver columns, according to what is said in the Canticle of Canticles: *He made columns of silver* [Song 3:10]; for which reason Moses placed five columns at the opening of the Tabernacle when entering it, and four columns in front of the oracle, that is, the Holy of Holies; this is explained in the sixth part, under the heading, *On the season of Advent.*[27] Moreover, while there might be several columns in the church, nonetheless we say there are seven, according to what is written: *Wisdom has built herself a house; she has hewn seven columns* [Prov 9:1]; and, since the bishops ought to be filled with the sevenfold grace of the Holy Spirit, James and John, as the Apostle says, were seen as columns [cf. Gal 2:9]. The bases of the columns are the Apostles, supporting the bishops and the universal fabric of the Church. The heads of the columns are the minds of the bishops and teachers; just as the members of the body are directed by the head, our words and deeds are directed by our minds. The capitals of the columns are the words of sacred Scripture upon which we must meditate and which we are obliged to follow.

28. The pavement of the church is the foundation of our faith; that is, in the spiritual Church, the foundation is Christ's poor ones, namely those who are poor in spirit, who humble themselves in all things, which

is why their humility is likened to pavement. On the other hand, the pavement, which is tread upon by the feet of the common people, represents the Church sustained by any of their labors.

29. The beams, which join the Lord's house, are the princes of the world or the preachers who defend the unity of the Church, one by their words, the other by their deeds.

30. The stalls [*reclinatoria*] in the church signify the contemplatives who remain at rest in God without offense, who, on account of their great holiness and the clarity of the eternal life they contemplate, are compared to gold; for which reason in Canticles it says: *He made himself a seat of gold* [Song 3:10].

31. The timbers in the church are the preachers who spiritually sustain it. The ceiling and rafters are the preachers who adorn and reinforce it, about whom—because they are not putrefied by vice—in the same Canticles, the groom boasts, saying: *The timbers of our house are cedars; the rafters are cypresses* [Song 1:17]. God built himself a house of living stones and incorruptible wood, according to what is written: *King Solomon made himself a carriage of wood from Lebanon* [Song 3:9]; that is, Christ, from the chastity of his pure saints. This is discussed elsewhere, under the heading, *On pictures.*[28]

The chancel, that is, the head of the church, which is lower than the rest of the body of the Church, mystically signifies how much humility ought to be among the clergy or bishops, according to that which is written: *The greater you are, humble yourself in all things* [Sir 3:20]. The grating that divides the altar from the choir signifies the separation of the celestial from the terrestrial realm. The chancel and the wall [*paribulum*] going around the choir are discussed under the heading, *On pictures.*[29]

32. The stall, on which one is seated in the choir, signifies that the body of anyone needs to be refreshed, because a body that lacks intervals of rest will not be a durable one.

33. The pulpit in the church is the life of the perfected and it is so-named [*pulpitum*] as if to say that it is set forth in a public place [*publicum*]; and indeed, we read in 2 Chronicles, chapter 6: *Solomon made a brazen scaffold, placing it in the middle of the Temple, and stood upon it* [2 Chr 6:13], and extending his hand, he spoke to the people of God. Ezra also made a wooden step from which to speak, and when he was on it, he stood above the whole people [cf. Ezra 8:4–5].

34. The rood-loft [*analogium*] is so called because the Word of God is read and proclaimed in it; *logos* is a Greek word, which means "rea-

son." It is also called an ambo from *ambiendo*, "to surround," because it surrounds and encloses him who has entered it; this is discussed in the fourth part, under the heading, *On the Gospel*.[30]

35. The clock [*horalogium*], according to which the liturgical hours are read, that is, when the community is assembled, signifies the diligence that the priests must have in reciting the canonical hours at the appointed time, according to what is written: *Seven times a day I will praise You* [Ps 118:164].

36. The roof tiles, which repel rain from the Lord's house, are the soldiers who protect the church from pagans and other enemies.

37. The spiral stairs, modeled after the Temple of Solomon, are the passageways secretly existing between the walls, through which we secretly receive the understanding of each of the mysteries, which things are known only to those who are climbing towards the celestial realm. The steps, which lead to the altar, are discussed in the next chapter.

38. The sacristy—the place where the sacred vessels are stored, or the place where the priest puts on the sacred vestments—signifies the womb of the most blessed Mary, in which Christ clothed Himself with the sacred vestment of His flesh. The priest processes to the people from the place where he put on his vestments because Christ, proceeding from the womb of the Virgin Mary, came into the world. The place where the bishop is seated is higher up, as discussed in the second part, in the treatise *On the bishop*.[31]

39. Near the altar, which signifies Christ, a basin or small tub is placed, which represents Christ's mercy, in which his hands are washed to show that in Baptism or Penance, which this represents, we are cleansed of the filth of our sins, a practice taken from the Old Testament. We read in Exodus chapters 30 and 40, that Moses made a bronze vessel with its own base that was placed in the Tabernacle, in which the priest Aaron and his sons could wash before ascending to the altar so that they could offer incense on it [cf. Ex 30:18; Ex 39:40].

40. The lamps that are lit in the church represent Christ, according to what is written: *I am the light of the world* [Jn 8:12], and John: *It was the true light*, etc. [Jn 1:9]. Also, the lamps in the church represent the Apostles and other teachers with whose teachings the Church shines like the sun and the moon, about which the Lord said: *You are the light of the world* [Mt 5:14], that is, the example of good works. Thus he admonished them, saying: *Let your light shine among men* [Mt 5:16]. The Church is illuminated according to the precept of the Lord, which is why in Exodus chapter 27, we read: *Order the sons of Aaron to offer oil*

from the purest olive tree so that the lamp will always be burning in the Tabernacle of testimony [Ex 27:20; Ex 40:12]; this is treated in the following book, under the heading *On the acolyte*.[32] Moses also made seven lamps, which are the seven gifts of the Holy Spirit, which in the night-time of this world illuminate the darkness of our own blindness; and they are placed upon candelabra because the spirit of wisdom and understanding, the spirit of counsel and fortitude, the spirit of knowledge and piety, the spirit of the fear of the Lord [cf. Isa 11:2; Isa 61:1], all rested on Christ, who preached forgiveness to those held captive in sin. The multitude of lamps in the church represents the multitude of graces among the faithful.

41. In many places a triumphal cross is placed in the middle of the church to denote that we love our redeemer from the depth of our heart,[33] who, according to Solomon, offered his body, *with deep charity* [Song 3:10], on account of the daughters of Jerusalem; and thus, all who see this sign of victory sing: "Hail, salvation of all the world, tree of life!"[34] And this is done so that the love of God that dwells in us—our God, who in order to redeem His servants, handed over His only son[35]—will never be handed over into oblivion, but rather we will imitate Christ's cross. Moreover, the cross is held high to designate Christ's victory. This is discussed where the *Consecration of a church* is treated.[36] Why the interior but not the exterior of a church is decorated is discussed in the treatise, *On pictures*.[37]

42. The cloister, just as Sicardus the Bishop of Cremona says in his *Mitrale*,[38] takes its origin from the watchmen or guards of the Levites around the Tabernacle, or from the entryway of the priests, or from Solomon's doorway to the Temple. For the Lord decreed to Moses that the Levites should not be numbered among the multitude of the people, but that they be appointed to carry and care for the Tabernacle of the Testimony. And on account of this precept of the Lord, when the divine mysteries are being performed, the clerics in church should stand apart from the laity. For this reason, the Council of Mainz decreed that the part of the church separated from the altar by the chancel is reserved only for clerics chanting the psalms.[39] Thus the Temple represents the Church triumphant, while the cloister signifies the celestial paradise where there will be one heart in the love and will of God, where everything will be held in common by everyone, since whoever has less for himself will rejoice for him who has more, because God will be all things for all people [cf. 1 Cor 15:28]. Therefore, the religious living commu-

nally in the cloister rise for the service of God,[40] leaving behind all worldly possessions and leading a common life.

43. The diversity of work areas[41] and offices in the cloister is the diversity of dwellings with their diverse rewards in the heavenly kingdom, since the Lord said: *In my Father's house there are many dwellings* [Jn 14:2]. In the moral sense, the cloister is the soul's contemplation, where it retreats when it separates itself from the carnal thoughts of the crowd and only meditates on celestial things. In this cloister there are four ramparts [*latera*]: contempt for self, contempt for the world, love of neighbor, and love of God. And every one of those walls has its own order of columns; contempt for self has humility of mind, affliction of the body, humility of speech, and other similar things; and the foundation of all of these columns in the cloister is patience. The diversity of work areas is the diversity of virtues; the chapter room is the secret area of the heart, as discussed in the fifth part, under the heading, *On prime*;[42] the refectory is the love of holy meditation; the cellar, sacred Scripture; the dormitory, a clean conscience; the oratory, a spotless life; the garden of trees and herbs, the accumulation of virtues, a well of living waters, the pouring out of blessings, which soothes those thirsting here, and in the future life will completely quench their thirst.

44. The episcopal seats, which according to the arrangement of Blessed Peter were consecrated in each of the ancient cities—as discussed in the prologue of the second part[43]—on account of the devotion of our ancestors, were not dedicated to the memory of Confessors but were built to honor the Apostles and Martyrs, and especially in honor of the Blessed Virgin Mary.

45. As for the rest, we assemble in the church to ask for the forgiveness of our offenses, and we persevere in the divine services—as discussed in the prologue of the fifth part[44]—and there we hear how to discern both good and evil things, and we learn and obtain our understanding of God; and we go there to eat the Lord's Body.

46. In the convent of the church, men and women live separate from each other, which, according to Bede, we accept as being derived from an ancient custom; and it comes from the time when Joseph and Mary lost their son, since each of them, who could not see Him, thought that He was with the other.[45] The cause, then, of this separation is that if the flesh of a man and woman are brought more closely together, they are enflamed with lust; thus when we ought to mourn for our sins, it is necessary for us to avoid those things that foster our sins and the carnal

delights. The men remain in the southern part, the women in the northern or northeast part in order to show that the stronger saints ought to stand against the greater temptations of this world, the weaker ones against the lesser temptations; or the stronger or firmer sex ought to be situated in a more open place, since, according to the Apostle: *God is faithful and will not let you suffer to be tempted beyond what you can endure* [1 Cor 10:13]. To this also can be applied that John saw a strong angel who placed his right foot on the sea [cf. Rev 10:2], for the stronger members are put against the greater dangers. And according to others, the men are in the front part and the women in the inner part since man is the head of the woman and therefore her leader [cf. Eph 5:23].

47. A woman also ought to have her head veiled in church because she is not the image of God [cf. 1 Cor 11:3–7]; and because through her, the transgression against God was begun, therefore in church, out of reverence for the priest who is Christ's vicar, she ought to have her head covered and not unveiled before him just as she would before her judge, on account of the original charge for which she is accused; neither, on account of the same reverence, does she have the power to speak in church before him [cf. 1 Cor 11:13–14]. In times past, though, men and women, growing their hair long, used to look at each other in church with bare heads, glorying in their own hair, which was shameful.

48. The Apostle showed what sort of speech should take place in church when he says: *Speak to one another in psalms, hymns, and spiritual canticles* [Eph 5:18]; and so superfluous speech should be avoided, according what is said by Chrysostom: "When you are about to enter the palace of the King, compose your demeanor and your gait, for the angels are present, since the Lord's house is full of incorporeal powers."[46] And the Lord said to Moses, and the angel to Joshua: *Remove your sandals from your feet; the place in which you stand is holy* [Ex 3:5; Josh 5:16].

49. Finally, it should be noted that those fleeing from bloody crimes to a consecrated church—so long as they did not commit them inside or outside the church—are defended by it, lest a life or limb be lost. And so we read that Joab fled into the Tabernacle and was seized at the corner of the altar [cf. 1 Chr 2:28]. The same privilege applies in an unconsecrated church in which the Divine Offices are celebrated.[47]

50. Still, reception of the Body of Christ by such people does not defend them, nor does fleeing to it offer defense, because this privilege is granted to churches, which is why it cannot be carried over to other

things, and why it is food for the soul and not the body; thus, it frees the soul and not the body.

51. There are three reasons why churches can be moved from one place to another.[48] First, on account of persecution; second, on account of the difficulty posed by the location (suppose, for example, on account of the inclemency of the weather); third, they are oppressed by the commerce of wicked men, and in this case, the approval of the pope or a bishop is required. Why those who are entering the church protect themselves with the sign of the cross is treated in the prologue of the fifth part.[49]

{ 2 }

ON THE ALTAR

1. There are three reasons why there is an altar in a church, as will be noted in the discussion of its dedication. It should be known, as it is written, that first Noah, then Abraham, Isaac, and Jacob built altars; these are understood to be nothing more than stones that were piled up, upon which they slaughtered the sacrifices and burnt them by placing fire on them. Moses also made an altar of *shittim* wood, and this was made into an altar of incense that he furnished with the purest gold, as can be read in Exodus chapters 25, 27, and 30, where the form of this altar is also set forth. Solomon, as stated in III Kings, chapter 7, near the end [1 Chr 7:28], also constructed a golden altar. The modern altars, which are erected with four corners, are derived from these ancient fathers; some of them are constructed from one stone, others from many stones.

2. Still, at different times we find the terms *altaria* and *arae* used indiscriminately; there is, nevertheless, a difference between the two. For "altar [*altare*]" can be taken to mean a "higher thing [*alta res*]" or "elevated hearth [*alta ara*],"[1] on which the priests burnt incense; *ara* can be taken to mean "vacant space [*area*]," that is, a level plane, or it can be derived from "flame [*ab ardore*]," because in that place sacrifices used to burn.

3. And note that in Scripture we read that there are multiple types of altars, namely, a higher and lower, or interior and exterior, whose parts each have a twofold sense. The higher altar is the Triune God, about which is written: *You shall not ascend my altar by steps* [Ex 20:26]. And the higher altar is the Church triumphant, about which is said: *Then you shall place your bull on the altar* [Ps 50:21]. The lower altar is the Church

militant, about which is said: *If you make an altar of stone for me, you shall not build it from cut stones* [Ex 20:25]. The low altar is also the table of the Temple, about which is said: *Decree a day of solemnity, [processing] with thick boughs to the horns of the altar* [Ps 117:27]; and in III Kings, chapter 7, it says that Solomon made a golden altar [cf. 1 Chr 7:48]. The interior altar is a pure heart, which is discussed later on. The interior altar is also our faith in the Incarnation, concerning which it is decreed in Exodus: *An altar of earth you shall make for me* [Ex 20:24]. The exterior altar is the altar of the cross; this is the altar of the holocaust on which the evening sacrifice was burnt, for which reason it says in the Canon of the Mass: "We pray that your angel may take this sacrifice to your altar in heaven," etc.[2] The exterior altar is also the ecclesiastical sacraments, about which is written: *Your altars, O Lord of virtues,* etc. [Ps 83:4].

Moreover, the altar is the mortification of the body or of the heart in which our carnal distractions are overcome by the fervor of the Holy Spirit. Second, the altar signifies the spiritual Church, and the four corners of the altar signify the four regions of the world through which the Church has spread. Third, it signifies Christ, without whom no acceptable offering can be made to the Father, and so the Church is accustomed to offer prayers to the Father, through Christ. Fourth, it signifies the Body of the Lord, as noted in the sixth part, under the heading *On the day of preparation.*[3] Fifth, it signifies the table on which Christ ate and drank with His disciples.

4. We read in Exodus [cf. Ex 40] that the Testimony, that is the tablets on which the Testament was written, was placed in the Ark of the Covenant or Testament; one can say that the Testimony exists wherever it is has been placed, and this can be proven when the Scriptures revive the natural law in the heart of man, upon which it has already been written. A full portion of manna was also placed in a golden urn to testify that the bread given to the sons of Israel came from heaven; and also the staff of Aaron, as proof that all power comes from the Lord God, and the Book of Deuteronomy, as proof of the pact by which the people said: we will do everything that the Lord has told us. For this reason it was called the Ark of the Covenant or Testament, and on account of this the Tabernacle was called the Tabernacle of the Testament. On top of the Ark a propitiation was offered [cf. Ex 25:17], about which we will speak in the prologue of the fourth part.[4] In imitation of this practice, in some churches they place on the altar an ark or tabernacle in which the Body of the Lord or the relics of Saints are deposited. The Lord also decreed

that a portable candelabrum of the purest gold be made [cf. Ex 25:31]. We also read in III Kings, chapter 8, that in the Ark of the Covenant, there was nothing except the two stone tablets that Moses placed in it on Mount Horeb when the Lord completed a pact with the sons of Israel when they were led out of the land of Egypt [cf. 1 Chr 8:9].

5. And note that at the time of Pope Sylvester, the Emperor Constantine constructed the Lateran Basilica, in which he placed the Ark of the Covenant that the Emperor Titus had carried off from Jerusalem, and the gold candelabrum with the seven branches. In that Ark were the following things: golden rings and poles; the tablets of the Testament; the staff of Aaron; manna; barley bread; a golden urn; seamless vestments; the reed; the vestments of Saint John the Baptist; and the scissors with which John the Evangelist was tonsured.

6. Thus, if a man has an altar, table, candelabrum and ark, he is a temple of God. It is, moreover, necessary for him to have an altar where he can properly offer and properly share his goods. The altar is our heart, on which we must make our offering, for which reason in Exodus the Lord decreed: *You shall offer a holocaust on an altar* [cf. Ex 20:24], because works kindled with the flame of charity should proceed from the heart. "Holocausts" are so called from *holon*, which means "entire," and *cauma*, which means "conflagration," as if to say "totally consumed by flame."[5] On this same altar we must properly offer and properly share our offerings. We properly offer when we bring to perfection the good which we intend. But we do not properly share our goods if we do not do good with discernment, because often a man thinks he is doing good but he is doing evil, and often he does good while on the other hand doing evil, and thus the same man can build or destroy. But we properly share our goods when we attribute the good that we do not to ourselves, but to God alone.

7. A man must also have a table where he can consume the bread of the words of God; we understand the table to be sacred Scripture, about which the Psalmist says: *You have prepared a table for me in front of those who oppress me* [Ps 22:5], that is, You have given me Scripture against the temptations of the Devil. It is then necessary that we have this table, that is, that we store it in our mind, so that there we can receive the bread of the words of God; in speaking about the failure of this bread Jeremiah says: *The little ones seek bread and there is no one who can break it for them* [Lam 4:4].

8. A man must also have a candelabrum so that it can shine with his good works. The candelabrum that shines outside is the good work that

inflames others through this good example, about which is written: *No one lights a lamp and places it under a measure, but on top of a lamp stand* [Lk 11:33]. The lamp, according to the word of the Lord, is a good intention, because he said: *The lamp is your eye* [Lk 11:34]; the eye truly is the intention. We should not put a lamp under a bushel but on top of a candlestick, because if we have a good intention we should not hide it, but put our good work in the light of day and show its example for others to see.

9. A man must also have an ark, which comes from the word "enclose [*ab arcendo*]."[6] An ark can also be called discipline, or the religious life[7] through which our offenses can be kept far away from us. Now in the ark there was a staff, the tablets of the Law, and manna, since in the religious life there must be the staff of correction so that the body can be chastised, and the tablets of love so that God can be loved; in the tablets were written the commandments which pertain to the love of God. There must also be the manna of the divine first fruits, that we might taste and see how sweet God is, because His affairs are good [cf. Prov 31:18], according to what is written in Proverbs, about the strong woman: *She tasted and saw because it is good* [cf. Prov 31:18].[8]

Thus, that we might be the temple of God, we have in us an altar for our offerings, lest we appear before God empty-handed, just as is written in Ecclesiasticus: *You shall not appear in the presence of your God empty-handed* [Sir 35:6]. Let us have a table for our refreshment, lest we become faint on our journey, like those who are fasting, according to the Gospel: *If we send them fasting, they will become faint on the way* [Mk 8:3]. Let us have a candelabrum for our good work, lest we become idle, according to what is written in Ecclesiasticus: *Idleness has taught much evil* [Sir 33:29]. Let us have an ark, lest we appear to be sons of Belial [or Satan], that is, without a yoke and undisciplined, for discipline is necessary according to the Psalm: *Take hold of discipline, lest God becomes angry with you at any time* [Ps 2:12]. These things and the other decorations for the altar are discussed in the next treatise.[9]

10. He builds this altar who furnishes his heart with true humility and other virtues, for which reason Gregory says: "He who assembles the virtues without humility is like one who carries dust in his open hand against the wind."[10] The altar is understood to be our heart, as stated where the dedication of an altar is treated;[11] it is in the middle of the body just as the altar is in the middle of the church. In Leviticus the following is decreed by the Lord concerning the altar: *The fire in my altar shall always blaze* [Lev 6:12].

11. The fire is charity, the altar is our pure heart; the fire will always blaze on the altar because charity will always inflame our heart, and so Solomon says in the Song of Songs: *Many waters cannot extinguish charity* [Song 8:7], because it always blazes and cannot be extinguished. According to the Prophet [cf. Ps 117:27], make a day of joy in your gathering together, or in your pressing together up to the corner of the altar, because your recollections of this day will become a feast day for you. The Apostle, touching on this, shows us the most excellent path [cf. 1 Cor 12:31]; he said that the most excellent path is charity, because she is above all the other virtues, and whoever possesses charity has all the other virtues [cf. Col 3:14]. This is an abbreviated version of what the Lord did when He was on earth; I would add that it is so brief that He might say: "Have charity and do whatever you wish, because the entire Law and Prophets depend upon those two commandments" [cf. Mt 22:40]. Also, we understand the altar to be the soul of anyone, built up by the Lord from living stones, namely from various and diverse virtues.

12. Furthermore, the white linens that cover the altar designate the flesh or the humility of the Savior; they are whitened with great effort just as the flesh of Christ, born of the earth, that is born of Mary, came to the resurrection and the purity and joy of immortality through many tribulations, about which the Son exults to the Father, saying: *You have taken off my sackcloth and surrounded me with joy* [Ps 29:12]. The vested altar is the soul joined to the immortal and incorruptible body. Again, the clean white cloths covering the altar represent the pure heart when it is adorned with good works, for which reason Apocalypse says: *Be clothed in white vestments lest the shame of your nakedness be evident* [Rev 3:18]; and Solomon: *At all times let your vestments be white* [Eccl 9:8], that is, let your works be clean. For it would hardly be of any advantage for one ascending the altar to have the highest dignity and the basest life, and so Blessed Bernard says: "It is a monstrous thing when the first seat is taken by someone of lowest life; the highest grade is occupied by someone of low status; the greatest authority is given to an unstable character."[12] The silken covers placed on the altar are the diverse virtues with which the soul is furnished. Moreover, the vestments with which the altar is furnished are the Saints, as explained in the following chapter. The beginning and end of the Mass are done on the right side of the altar; the middle portion is done on the left side, for the reasons stated in the fourth part, in the treatise, *On the movements of the priest.*[13]

Pope Sixtus decreed that Mass must be celebrated on an altar,[14] which beforehand was not always done. Our forefathers used to make their altars in a hollow on account of what they read in Ezekiel, chapter 43 [cf. Ezek 43:13], that the altar of the Lord was made in a ditch, done this way, according to Gregory, "Lest their holocausts be overturned and scattered by the wind."[15] It also says in chapter 40 [cf. Ezek 40:43], that around the inside edges there were ledges.

13. As for the rest, the steps by which the altar is ascended spiritually represent the Apostles and Martyrs of Christ, who on account of their love for Him, shed their blood; the bride in the Canticle of love calls the seat purple [cf. Song 3:10].[16] The steps also display the fifteen virtues, which are signified by the fifteen steps that were ascended in the Temple of Solomon, and by the Prophet, in the fifteen successive Psalms in which are demonstrated that the blessed man has arranged those fifteen steps in his heart.[17] Jacob saw this ladder, whose highest part touched the heavens [cf. Gen 28:12]. These steps are understood to correspond with the steps of virtue by which the altar—that is, Christ—is approached, according to what the Psalm says: *And they shall go from virtue to virtue* [Ps 83:8]. And Job: *Through each of my steps I shall proclaim Him* [Job 31:37]. We also read in Exodus: *You shall not ascend my altar on the steps lest your shamefulness be revealed* [Ex 20:26], for perhaps the ancients did not yet use garments that covered their lower parts. In the Council of Toledo it was decreed that a cleric who, on account of sorrow, despoils an altar, or a strips a sacred image of its coverings, or covers them with vestments of mourning, or girds them with thorns, or extinguishes the lamps in the church, shall be deposed.[18] But if his church had been unjustly deprived of its rights, it was permitted for him to do this, on account of his sorrow, which according to some, is why on the day of the Lord's Passion, and as a sign of sorrow, the altars are stripped; but nevertheless, nowadays, the Council of Lyons has condemned this practice.[19] Finally, altars which are constructed on account of visions or after the empty revelations of men are entirely forbidden.[20]

ON THE PICTURES, CURTAINS, AND ORNAMENTS
OF THE CHURCH

1. The pictures and ornaments in the church are the readings and scriptures of the laity; thus Gregory says: "It is one thing to worship a picture, another thing to learn, by means of the picture, the story that should be adored; for what texts supply to those who read, the picture shows to the illiterate viewers, for in the picture the ignorant see what they ought to follow, and the unlettered, by looking at it, read."[1] It is a fact that the Chaldeans worship fire and compel others to do the same, while burning other idols. The pagans worship images, and icons and other idols, which the Saracens do not do, since neither do they have images nor do they look upon them, prompted by this text: *You shall not make for yourself anything in the shape of things in the heavens or on the earth, or under the waters, or beneath the earth* [Ex 20:4]; and from other authorities, which they unhesitatingly follow, they indignantly attack us on this point. But we do not worship images, nor do we call them gods, nor do we place our hope of salvation in them, because this would be idolatry, but we venerate them for the memory and remembrance of things done long ago, hence the verse:

"You who pass, honor with a bow, the image of Christ
Worship not the image but what it represents
To call it God is baseless for him who attributes divinity to it
For it was once a material stone, sculpted by hand, into an image
And the image upon which you gaze is neither God nor man
But it is both God and man which this sacred image represents."[2]

2. The Greek [Christians], too, use images, painting them, as they say, only from the navel upwards, and never below, so that any occasion for

foolish thoughts is removed. And they never make sculpted images, on account of what is written in Exodus 20: *You shall not make carved figures or images* [Ex 20:4]. Again, Leviticus 26: *You shall not make idols or graven images* [Lev 26:1]; again, Deuteronomy 4: *Lest you be deceived and make for yourselves a graven image* [Deut 4:16]; again: *You shall not make for yourselves gods of gold or silver* [Ex 20:23]; again, the Prophet: *The idols of the gentiles are gold and silver, the handiwork of men* [Ps 113:12]; *their makers shall become like them, as all who put their trust in them* [Ps 113:16]; *all who worship idols and glory in their images are confounded* [Ps 96:7]. Again, Moses said to the people of Israel: *Lest by your error you are deceived and worship those things which the Lord your God created* [Deut 4:19].

3. So it was that King Hezekiah broke to pieces the golden serpent that Moses had set up, because the people, contrary to the precept of the Law, burnt incense before it [cf. 2 Chr 18:4].

4. From these and similar authorities, the overuse of images is prohibited. And indeed, the Apostle says in 1 Corinthians: *We know that an idol is nothing in this world, and that there is no God but the one God* [1 Cor 8:4]. The simple and the infirm, by an excessive and indiscreet use of images, can be drawn into idolatry; for which reason it says in Wisdom chapter 14: *There shall be no respect for the idols of the nations, because they made the creatures of God hateful, and made the temptation of men's souls, and snares for the feet of the unwise* [Wis 14:11]. But it is not blameworthy to make moderate use of pictures to represent those wicked things that should be avoided and the good things that should be imitated. And so the Lord said to Ezekiel: *Go in, and see the worst abominations that these men do. And going in, he saw the likeness of reptiles and animals, and the abomination, and all the idols of the house of Israel depicted on the wall* [Ezek 8:9–10]. This is why Gregory, explicating this in book 2 of his *Pastoral Care*, says: "When the shapes of external objects are drawn within, it is as if they were painted in the heart, whenever the faint images are thought about carefully."[3] Again, to the same Ezekiel it was said: *Take a tile and place it before yourself and draw the city of Jerusalem on it* [Ezek 4:1].

But those things just said, that images are the letters of the laity, opposes this Gospel text: *They have, he said, Moses and the Prophets; let them hear them* [Lk 16:29]. This is discussed in the fourth part, on the fourth portion of Canon of the Mass, under the word "servitutis."[4] The Council of Agde[5] prevents the creation of pictures in churches, and the painting of what is worshiped and adored on the walls; but Gregory says that pictures are not to be destroyed on the pretext that they are not to be adored.⁶ Indeed, pictures seem to move the soul more than texts. Through pictures certain deeds are placed before the eyes, and they seem to be happening in the present time, but with texts, the deeds seem to be only a story heard, which moves the soul less, when the thing is recalled by the memory. For this reason we do not show as much reverence towards books as we do to images and pictures.

5. Some pictures or images are on top of the church, such as the cock and the eagle; others are outside the church, namely, outside and in front of the church, such as the ox and the lion; others are inside, such as icons, statues, and diverse types of pictures and sculptures, which can be depicted on vestments, or on walls, or in windows—concerning which other things were discussed in the treatise *On the church*.⁷ This practice is taken from the Tabernacle of Moses and the Temple of Solomon. For Moses engraved images, and Solomon engraved and painted, and adorned the walls with sculptures and paintings.

6. It should also be known that the image of the Savior is depicted in church in three suitable ways, namely: either seated on a throne, or hanging fastened to His cross, or resting on the bosom of His mother. Because John the Baptist pointed to Him and said: *Behold the Lamb of God* [Jn 1:29], for that reason some have depicted Christ in the form of a lamb. Because that old form has passed away, and since Christ is true man, Pope Hadrian says that He must be depicted in human form.⁸ Therefore the "Lamb of God" must not in principle be depicted on the cross, but His human form; but this does not hinder the depiction of a lamb in a lower or less prominent part of the picture, since He is the true Lamb who takes away the sins of the world [cf. Jn 1:29].

7. In these and diverse other manners the image of the Savior is depicted, on account of the diverse significations it bears. Now when He is depicted in the cradle, this recalls His Nativity; depicted on His mother's bosom, His boyhood; a painting or a sculpture of His cross recalls His Passion, and sometimes the sun and moon are depicted on the cross, as if representing an eclipse, which signifies His patience; when depicted ascending steps, His Ascension is recalled; a picture of Him on a throne or a lofty seat indicates His present majesty and power, as if He said: *All power in heaven and on earth is given to Him* [Mt 28:18], according to what is said: *I saw the Lord sitting on an exalted throne* [Isa 6:1], that is, the Son of God reigning over the angels, as it says: *Who is seated over the Cherubim* [2 Chr 19:15]. Sometimes He is painted as He was seen by Moses and Aaron, Nadab and Abihu, namely on the mountain, and under His feet is a work of sapphire, as it were, like heaven in its clear

serenity [cf. Ex 24:10]. And since just as Luke says: *Then they shall see the Son of Man coming in a cloud with great power and majesty* [Lk 21:27], therefore He is sometimes painted surrounded by angels, who always serve and assist Him, who have six wings, according to Isaiah, who says: *The seraphim stood beneath it; each had six wings, and with two they veiled his face, with two his feet, and with two they hovered about* [Isa 6:2].

8. The angels are also represented in the flower of their youthful age, since they never grow old. Sometimes the archangel Michael is painted around Him, trampling the dragon under foot, according to what John says: *There was a war in heaven; Michael fought with the dragon* [Rev 12:7], which was a war of dissension among the angels, and the confirmation of those that were good and the downfall of the wicked ones, or in the present Church, the persecution of the faithful. Sometimes the twenty-four Elders are painted around Him, according to the vision of John [cf. Rev 4:4], with white robes and golden crowns, by which are signified the teachers of the Old and New Law; they are twelve each on account of faith in the Trinity which they preached through the four corners of the world, or twenty-four, on account of their works and their observance of the Gospels. If lamps are added, they represent the gifts of the Holy Spirit; if a sea of glass, Baptism is implied.

9. Sometimes He is surrounded by paintings of the four animals, following the vision of Ezekiel and the same John: *The face of a man and the face of a lion on the right; the face of an ox on the left and the face of an eagle above the four* [Ezek 1:10; cf. Rev 4:6–8]. These are the four Evangelists, for which reason they are painted with books near their feet, because what they have accomplished in their minds and in their works, they have taught others by their words and writings. Matthew is cast as a human figure and Mark has the figure of a lion; both of them are placed at the right side, because the nativity and resurrection of Christ were the universal joy of all people, and so in the Psalm it says: *And in the morning, gladness* [Ps 29:6].

Luke is the ox, because he began his account from the priesthood of Zachary, and paid special attention to the Passion and sacrifice of Christ, and the ox is an animal especially fit for priestly sacrifice. Luke is compared to the ox on account of its two horns, as if to say they contain the two Testaments, and the four hoofs, as if to say they contain the sentences of the four Gospels. The ox is also, figuratively, Christ, who was the ox sacrificed for us; therefore, the ox is placed on the left side, because the death of Christ was the sorrow of the Apostles. This topic, and how Mark should be depicted, is treated in the seventh part, under the heading *On the Evangelists.*[9]

John is given the figure of an eagle because flying to the greatest heights, he said: *In the beginning was the Word* [Jn 1:1]. This also signifies Christ, whose youth, like that of the eagle, is renewed, because rising from the dead, He flourished and entered heaven; but here the eagle is not depicted next to Christ but above, because it represents the Ascension and it proclaims the Word in the presence of God. But how any of these four creatures might have four faces and four wings, and how they can be depicted, is treated in the seventh part, under the heading *On the Evangelists*, where this is more broadly covered.[10]

10. Sometimes the Apostles—who were His witnesses by word and deed, to the ends of the earth—are painted around Him, or more preferably, below. And they are depicted with long hair, as Nazarites, that is, holy men. There was a law among the Nazarites, that from the time of their separation from the life of common men, a razor would not pass over their heads. Sometimes they are depicted in the form of twelve sheep, since they were killed like sacrificial lambs on account of the Lord; sometimes the twelve tribes of Israel are represented when they are depicted in the form of twelve sheep. Sometimes, however, many or few sheep are depicted around the seat of majesty, but this represents something else, according to the text of Matthew, chapter 25, near the end: *When the Son of man shall come in His majesty, then He shall sit on the seat of His majesty, placing the sheep on His right and the goats on His left* [Mt 25:31]. How Bartholomew and Andrew ought to be depicted is discussed in the seventh part, under their feasts.[11]

11. And note that the Patriarchs and Prophets are painted with scrolls in their hands, and some of the Apostles are depicted with books and some with scrolls. This is clearly because before the coming of Christ, the faith was shown figuratively, and many things remained unclear; to represent this, the Patriarchs and Prophets are painted with scrolls, as if to denote this imperfect knowledge. But since the Apostles were instructed perfectly by Christ, they can be shown with books, by which is suitably depicted their perfect knowledge. But because some of them put down in writing what they had learned, for the instruction of others, they are fittingly depicted as if they were teachers, with books in their hands, such as Paul, the Evangelists, Peter, James and Jude. But others, who wrote nothing that has survived or has been approved by the Church, are not depicted with books but with scrolls, as a sign of their preaching. For this reason the Apostle says to the Ephesians: *The Lord*

gave some as apostles, some as prophets, others as evangelists, others as pastors and teachers in the work of ministry [Eph 4:11–12].

12. But the Divine Majesty is sometimes depicted with a closed book in His hands, because no one was found worthy to open it, except the lion of Judah [cf. Rev 4:11; Rev 5:5]; and sometimes He is depicted with an open book, so that anyone can read in it that He is the light of the world, and the way, the truth, and the life, and the book of life [cf. Jn 1:4]. Why Paul is painted on the right and Peter on the left of the Savior is discussed in the seventh part, under the heading *On the Gospel.*[12]

13. John the Baptist is depicted as a hermit.

14. Martyrs are shown with the instruments of their pain—such as St. Lawrence on the grill, Stephen with the stones—and sometimes with palms, which signify victory, following the text: "The righteous shall flourish like a palm tree;"[13] just as the palm tree is verdant, so too shall their memory flourish. Thus it is that those who come from Jerusalem with palms in their hands bear them as a sign that they soldier for their King who was received with honor in Jerusalem with palms, and who afterwards, fighting in the same place with the Devil, emerged the victor and entered the palace of heaven in triumph with His angels, where the righteous shall flourish as palms, and they shall shine just as the stars.

15. Confessors are painted with their own insignia, such as mitered bishops, and hooded abbots, and sometimes with lilies, which represent chastity; doctors have books in their hands; virgins, following the Gospel, are shown with lamps.

16. Paul is shown with a book and a sword; with a book because he is a doctor, or on account of his conversion; with a sword because he was a soldier, and so the verse says: The sword is the ire of Paul; the book is the conversion of Saul.

17. Generally the images of the holy fathers are either painted on the walls of the church or on the back panels of the altar, or on sacred vestments, and in other various places, so that we might meditate continually, not indiscreetly or uselessly, on their acts and their sanctity. For this reason in Exodus [cf. Ex 28:15–29] it was decreed, by a divine command, that the breastplate of judgment be placed on Aaron's breast, bound with strings, since the priestly heart should never be occupied with fleeting thoughts, but should only be bound by reason. In the same breastplate, it was commanded, according to Gregory, that the names of the twelve patriarchs be carefully inscribed.[14]

18. Indeed, to carry the fathers imprinted on the breast is to dwell without intermission on the lives of the ancients. Thus, the priest walks

blamelessly when he continually bears with him the example of the fathers who preceded him; when he considers, without cease, the footprints of the saints, and represses illicit thoughts, lest he extend his foot past the limits of the work of prayer.

19. It should be carefully noted that Jesus is always depicted crowned, as if He said: *Come forth, sons of Jerusalem, and see King Solomon in the diadem with which his mother crowned him* [Song 3:11]. Christ was, moreover, triply crowned. First, by His mother, with the crown of mercy, on the day of His conception, which is a double crown, on account of what He had by nature and what was given to Him; therefore, it is also called a diadem, which is a double crown. Second, by His stepmother, in the day of His Passion, which is the crown of misery. Third, by His Father, with the crown of glory, on the day of His Resurrection, for which reason it says: *O Lord, You have crowned him with glory and honor* [Ps 8:6].[15] Lastly, He shall be crowned with the crown of power by His family, on the last day of revelation; He shall come with the elders of the earth, judging the world with equity. So, too, all the Saints are depicted crowned, as if He says: "Daughters of Jerusalem, come and see the Martyrs with the golden crowns with which the Lord has crowned them,"[16] and in the Book of Wisdom: *The just shall receive a kingdom of beauty, and a beautiful diadem from the hand of the Lord* [Wis 5:17].

20. Their crowns are depicted in the form of a round shield, because the saints benefit from the divine protection, and so they sing joyfully: *O Lord, You have crowned us with the shield of your approval* [Ps 5:13]. But the crown of Christ is distinguished from the crowns of saints by the figure of a cross, because through the battle standard of the cross, He achieved the glorification of His body, and earned for us freedom from captivity and the enjoyment of eternal life. When any prelate or Saint is depicted while alive, their crown is not in the form of a round shield but their crown is square, so that they may be shown to be thriving with the four cardinal virtues, just as we find in the legend of Blessed Gregory.[17]

21. Sometimes Paradise is depicted in churches, so that those gazing upon it are drawn to the delights of the eternal reward; and sometimes hell, that it might deter them with the terrors of that punishment; and sometimes flowers and trees, to represent the fruits of good works, springing from the roots of the virtues.

22. Now the variety of pictures denotes the variety of virtues. For to one is given the word of wisdom; to another, a word of knowledge, etc.

[cf. 1 Cor 12:8]. The virtues are depicted in the form of women because they soothe and nourish. Again, the ribbed ceilings, which are called vaults, which exist for the beauty of the Lord's house, are understood to be the simplest of Christ's servants, who adorn the Church not with their teaching but by their virtues alone. And the bas-relief sculptures seem to be coming out of the walls of the church, because when by such practice, the virtues come to the faithful—so that they seem to be naturally inborn in them—they are easily practiced in a multitude of works. How a synagogue should be depicted is discussed in the fourth part, under the title *On reverence*.[18] How the pallium of the Roman Pontiff is painted is discussed in the third part, under the title *On the pallium*.[19] How the year and the twelve zodiacal signs and months are depicted is discussed in the eighth part, and where the topic *On the month* is discussed.[20] But the diverse stories of the New and Old Testaments can be depicted according to the wishes of the painter, for "both painters and poets have always had equal power to do what they dare."[21]

23. Furthermore, the ornaments of the church consist of three types, namely, in the decoration of the church, the choir, and the altar. The decoration of the church consists of curtains and tapestries, silken or purple coverings, and other such things; the decoration of the choir consists of coverings, tapestries, floor coverings, and cushions; the coverings are specifically cloths that hang in the choir, behind the clergy; the floor coverings are things that are spread out under their feet; the tapestries are cloths that are spread out under foot, specifically for walking on, and especially for the feet of bishops who must walk over worldly things with their feet; the cushions are cloths that are placed on the seats or benches in the choir.

24. The decoration of the altar consists of cases, coverings, phylacteries, candelabra, crosses, gold fringes, banners, books, veils, and curtains.

25. And note that the case in which the consecrated hosts are preserved signifies the body of the glorious Virgin, about whom is spoken in the Psalm: *Ascend, O Lord, to your rest, You and the ark of your sanctification* [Ps 131:8]. The case is sometimes made of wood; sometimes of white ivory; sometimes of silver; sometimes of gold; sometimes of crystal; and according to these diverse varieties and properties the different graces of the Body of Christ itself are expressed. Again, the case itself, containing consecrated or unconsecrated hosts, signifies the human memory: for man ought continually to remember the reception of God's

gifts, both the temporal—which the unconsecrated hosts signify—and the spiritual—which are represented by the consecrated hosts. This was prefigured in the urn into which God decreed that the manna should be deposited, which though it was temporal, nevertheless prefigured our spiritual sacrifice, with God decreeing that it be a perpetual memorial for future generations, just as we read in Exodus [cf. Ex 16]. Moreover, the cases placed on the altar—which is Christ—are the Apostles and Martyrs; the coverings and vestments are the Confessors and Virgins or all the saints, about which the Prophet said to the Lord: *With these you shall be clothed with a vestment* [Isa 49:18]. This was discussed in the previous chapter.

26. There is also a phylactery of two sorts. A phylactery [*philaterium*] is a parchment on which the Ten Commandments of the Law were written, and the Pharisees used to carry a parchment of this sort in front of them as a sign of their piety, and so it says in the Gospel: *They enlarge their phylacteries* [Mt 23:5]. And phylactery comes from the word *philare*, which means "to guard or preserve," and *thorax*, which is "law." A phylactery [*philateria*] is also a small vase made of silver, gold or crystal, or of ivory, or things of this sort, in which the ashes or relics of saints are stored. When Elindius called the faithful "ash-like," because they saved their ashes, it was decreed in the Church, against his mockery, that such remains are honorably preserved in precious little vases;[22] and this name is taken from *philare*,[23] which is "to preserve," and *teron*,[24] which means "extremity," because in it is preserved some extremity from the saints' bodies; for example, a tooth, or a finger, or some other such thing. In some churches, a tabernacle is placed on the altar, as was discussed under the heading *On the altar*.[25]

27. There are two candelabra placed at the corners of the altar, to signify the joy of the two people [Jews and Gentiles] rejoicing in the Nativity of Christ; in the middle of the candelabrum is a cross, bearing small, lit torches, for the angel said to the shepherds: *I proclaim to you joy for all people, since today is born to you the savior of the world* [Lk 2:10–11], that is, the true Isaac, which means "laughter." The light from the candelabra is the faith of the people, since the Prophet said to the Jewish people: *Arise and illumine Jerusalem, since your light has come, and the glory of the Lord has come upon you* [Isa 60:1]. To the Gentiles the Apostle says: *For you once were in darkness, now you are light in the Lord* [Eph 5:8]. Now in the birth of Christ a new star appeared to the Magi, following the prophecy of Balaam: *A star shall arise*, he says, *from Jacob, and*

a staff shall come forth from Israel [Num 24:17]. More is said about this in the chapter *On the altar*.[26]

28. The candle snuffers or tongs for putting out the lamps are the divine words with which we cut through the letter of the Law and reveal its spiritual light, according to this: *You shall have so much of the oldest [crops] to consume that you shall have to discard the old to make way for the new* [Lev 26:10]. The vases in which the wicks are extinguished are the hearts of the faithful who are committed to observing the Law to the letter.

29. Again, the tongs, the pair of which is applied to the tooth of the flame, are the preachers who instruct us in the harmony of the pages of either Testament, and inflame us with the habits that create charity.

30. The trays [*scutra*], that is, the vases of equal dimensions from bottom to top, made to provide heat, are those doctors who do not hide the treasure of their heart, but from it offer both new and old things. They also do not place a lamp beneath a measure [cf. Lk 11:33] but on a candlestick, so that those who are in the house of the Lord may receive the light and zeal of the Holy Spirit.

31. The cross must be placed on the altar, and from there, the cross bearer carries it, by which is remembered that Simon of Cyrene carried the cross after lifting it from the shoulders of Christ. The cross is placed in the middle of the altar between two candelabra because Christ stands, in the Church, as the mediator between the two peoples [Jews and Gentiles]. For He is the cornerstone who made one from each of the two, to whom came the shepherds from Judea and the Magi from the east. More is said about this in the prologue of the fourth part,[27] and under the heading *On the procession of the priest to the altar*.[28]

32. The front of the altar is adorned with gold trim, according to Exodus chapters 25 and 27: *You shall make an altar for me; you shall make a garland to frame it or surround it, at a height of four digits* [cf. Ex 25:25; 27:1].[29] The altar sometimes signifies the heart of man, in which the sacrifice of true faith should be offered through contrition, and thus the gold trim signifies the concept of good works, with which our brow should be adorned that we may shine for others. Sometimes the altar signifies Christ, and then the gold fittingly represents the decoration of charity. Just as gold surpasses all metals, so too does charity all of the other virtues, and so the Apostle says to the Corinthians, chapter 1: *The greatest of these is charity* [1 Cor 13:13]. We should thus decorate our brow with the gold trim of charity, so that we may be prepared to lay

down our lives for Christ. Banners are also erected above the altar, so that the triumph of Christ is continually remembered in the church, through which we hope to triumph over the enemy.

33. The codex of the Gospels is also placed on the altar, since the Gospel was published by Him, that is, Christ, and He still provides testimony to us. Why this codex is decorated on the outside is discussed in the third part, under the heading *On the vestments of the Old Law*.[30] Finally, the vases and utensils in the Lord's house originated with Moses and Solomon, which were many and diverse in the Old Testament, just as we read in Exodus [cf. Ex 27–28]; they signified diverse things that we will not treat here for the sake of brevity.

34. It is fitting that everything that pertains to decoration of the church ought to be removed or covered during the season of Lent, which is done, according to some, on Passion Sunday, since from that point, the Divinity was hidden or veiled in Christ; for He handed Himself over to be seized and flogged as a man, as if He no longer had the power of the Divinity in Himself, and so in the Gospel of this day it says: *Jesus therefore hid Himself and went out of the Temple* [Jn 8:59]; therefore the crosses are covered, as if to say that they represent the power of His Divinity. Others do this from the first Sunday of Lent, since from that point, the Church begins to think of His Passion; and so during that time, the cross should not be carried in the church unless it is covered; and according to the custom of some places, two coverings or curtains are kept, one of which is placed around the choir and the other which is hung between the altar and the choir, lest those things which are in the Holy of Holies be seen. And the covering of the sanctuary and the cross signify the letter of the Law, that is, its carnal observance, or what was in the Old Testament, before the Passion of Christ, when the understanding of sacred Scripture was veiled, covered, and obscure, and those who lived during that time always had a veil before their eyes, that is, a shady knowledge. It also signifies that weapon placed before the door of Paradise, and since the carnal observance of this sort and the obscure law and the sword have been mitigated by the Passion of Christ, therefore the curtains and veils of this sort are removed on Good Friday. But since in the Old Testament there were cud-chewing animals and those with split hooves, like plowing oxen—that represent the discernment of the mystery of the Scriptures and understanding them spiritually—therefore, during Lent, only a small number of priests, to whom it is given to know the mystery of the reign of God, go behind the veil.

35. Concerning these things it should be noted that three types of veils are hung in church, namely, that which covers sacred things, that which divides the clergy from the sanctuary, and that which separates the clergy from the people. The first signifies the letter of the Law; the second denotes our unworthiness, since we are unworthy or rather powerless to enter Heaven; the third, the restraint of our carnal pleasure.

In the first—namely the curtains which are spread out on either corner of the altar, through which the priest enters the secret place [secretum], as will be discussed in the fourth part, under the heading *On the secret*[31]—is signified, just as we read in Exodus, chapter 34 [cf. Ex 34:33], that Moses placed a veil over his face because the sons of Israel were not able to bear the splendor of his face. And as the Apostle says, this veil remains, even to this day over the hearts of the Jews [cf. 2 Cor 3:15].

In the second, namely, the curtains that are spread out in front of the altar in Lent during Mass, is signified the veil that hung in the Tabernacle that divided the Holy of Holies from the sanctuary—as will be discussed in the prologue of the fourth part[32]—with which the Ark was veiled from the people. And it was made with admirable craftsmanship and distinguished by a variety of beautiful materials, a veil that was torn asunder in the Passion of the Lord [cf. Lk 23:45]; and today, following its example, the curtains are made with a variety of beautiful materials. More about the first curtain and how curtains should be made can be found in chapters 26, 35, and 36 of Exodus.

The third veil has its origins from the fact that in the primitive Church, the outward wall [paribolus], that is, the wall that went around the choir, was built up to the *apodiationem*,[33] which even now they still do in some churches; and this was done so that the people seeing the clergy singing would receive a good example.

36. Nevertheless, at this time a veil is almost always suspended or placed between the clergy and people, or a wall is put up, lest they be able to see each other, as if to say by this act: *Turn your eyes, lest they see vanity*, etc. [Ps 118:37]. But on Holy Saturday every veil is removed, since during the Lord's Passion, the veil of the Temple was torn in half, through which was revealed to us that the spiritual understanding of the Law, which had been hidden to that point, as we said previously, was revealed; and the doors of the kingdom of heaven were opened and the strength was given to us to prevail, unless we veil ourselves, unable to conquer the concupiscence of the flesh.

Nevertheless, the veil that divides the sanctuary from the clergy is retracted or elevated during Vespers on any Saturday during Lent, or when the Sunday Office is begun, so that the clergy can enter the sanctuary, since the Lord's day recalls the Resurrection.

37. This is, therefore, the practice in the six Sundays after Easter, because there was no time period in which there was not eternal joy [for the Resurrection]; a joy that is figurative, veiled by the heavens, which is what is signified by this veil. For that reason, we do not fast on Sundays, on account of the glory of the Lord's Resurrection. Now the first Sunday signifies the joy that our first parents had in Paradise, before the coming of sin. The second Sunday represents the joy that a few had on Noah's Ark, while all the others were drowned in the flood. The third, the joy that the sons of Israel had, while famine afflicted others in the time of Joseph. The fourth, the joy had by those who lived in peace under Solomon. The fifth, the joy of those returning from captivity in Babylon. The sixth, the joy that the disciples had from the Resurrection to the Ascension, when the bridegroom was with them in person.

38. In feasts with nine lessons[34] during Lent, that veil is lifted or raised. But this custom does not come from the establishment of the early Church, since at that time, no solemn feast was celebrated during Lent. But, if any feast occurred, regardless of the day on which it occurred, its commemoration took place on Saturday or Sunday, as found in the canon of Pope Martin,[35] and in Burchard, book 13;[36] and all of this was done on account of the sorrow of this season. Afterwards, the opposite custom took hold, namely, that a feast with nine lessons was solemnly celebrated on its own day; nevertheless, it was a day of fasting.

39. On feast days the curtains are spread out in churches to decorate them, so that through visible ornaments, we will be moved to the invisible ones; these curtains are often dyed with a variety of colors, as stated before, and the diversity of their colors denotes that man, who is the temple of God, ought to be decorated with a variety or diversity of virtues. A white curtain signifies purity of life; a red one, charity; green, contemplation; black, mortification of the flesh; gray, tribulation. And sometimes, we hang draperies of various colors on top of the white curtains, to denote that our heart ought to be purged of vices, and in it should be curtains of virtue and a variety of good works.

40. Furthermore, on the Feast of the Nativity of the Lord, some churches hang no draperies; some, cheap ones; others, good ones. The ones who hang none represent our shame; for if we have great joy for the birth of our Savior, we should nevertheless not be without shame for the fact that our sin was such that the Son of God Himself lowered Himself for us, taking the form of a slave; and on account of that, as if on the

day of His death, we do not solemnly celebrate with joy but we practice the strictest fast, when in fact, on the feast of the death of other Saints, we solemnly celebrate with joy, and we indulge ourselves with more food and drink, as we say in the sixth part, *On Holy Saturday*.[37] We are indeed ashamed that the Lord died on account of our sins, but the Saints suffered not because of our sins but for Christ. Those who hang cheap curtains symbolize that the Lord put on the form of a slave, and that He was wrapped up in cheap cloth on the day of His birth. Those who use good cloth show the joy that accompanies the birth of a king, and they show how we should be when receiving such a guest.

41. In some churches, the altar is decorated with costly coverings during Easter, and veils of three different colors are placed on top of them: red, gray, and black, which denote three time periods. When the first lesson and the response are finished, the black veil, which represents the time before the Law, is removed. When the second lesson and the response are finished, the gray veil, which represents the time under the Law, is removed. When the third is finished, the red one is removed, which represents the time of grace; by Christ's Passion He made available for us, in that time, access to the Holy of Holies and eternal glory. More is said about the coverings and vestments of the altar in the treatise, *On the altar*.[38]

42. On the principal solemn feast days the treasury[39] of a church is opened up publicly for three reasons. First, out of regard for security, namely, that it be made apparent how careful they must be in preserving those things in whose care they are entrusted. Second, on account of reverence for the solemnity. Third, in memory of their being offered to that church, namely, in memory of those who first offered them to that church. That the interior and not the exterior of the church is decorated on feast days mystically implies that all of its glory is internal. Certainly, the exterior might be deplorable, but the soul, which is the throne of God, shines, according to what is written: *I am black, but lovely* [Song 1:4],[40] and the Lord through the Prophet: *How splendid to me is my inheritance* [Ps 15:6]. The Prophet, also considering this, says: *O Lord, how I have loved the beauty of your house*, etc. [Ps 25:8][41], which faith, hope, and charity spiritually adorn. How the material and spiritual Church must be cleansed is discussed in the sixth part, under the headings *On Easter*[42] and on *Holy Thursday*.[43]

43. In some churches they keep ostrich eggs suspended, or something of this sort, which cause wonderment since they are so rarely seen, so that people are drawn to church and greatly touched by this sight. On

the other hand, some say that the ostrich is such a forgetful bird that she leaves her eggs in the sand, and after seeing a certain star, remembers where they are and goes to them and covers them over to keep them warm. The eggs are suspended in church to denote that man is alienated from God on account of sin; if at last he is illumined with a divine light, recalling his faults, he shall repent and return to Him, and through the vision of His grace, his sin is covered over. And in the same manner it says in Luke that the Lord looked at Peter after he denied Christ [cf. Lk 22:61].[44] These eggs are also suspended in church so that anyone contemplating them will recall that man easily forgets God unless illumined by the star, that is through the in-breathing of the grace of the Holy Spirit, he is called to return to Him through good works.

44. Now in the early Church the sacrifice was offered with wooden vessels and ordinary vestments, since then, the chalices were made of wood and the priests, of gold; now it is precisely the opposite. But Pope Zepherinus[45] decreed that they be offered in glass vessels; but because they were very fragile, Pope Urban[46] and the Council of Rheims[47] decreed that the sacrifice be offered in vessels of silver or gold; or on account of poverty, out of tin, since it does not rust, but not out of wood or copper. The vessel should not be made of glass on account of the danger of spilling the wine; neither should it be made of wood since it is a porous and spongy material that will absorb the Lord's Blood; neither should it be made of brass or of copper, since the strength of the wine mixed with rust would induce vomiting when drunk.

45. And note that the name for the cup [calix] is drawn from both the Old and New Testaments, and so Jeremiah says: *Babylon was a gold cup which made the whole world drunk* [Jer 51:7]; and David: *There is a chalice in the Lord's house full of spiced and foaming wine*[48] [Ps 74:9]; and in another place: *I will take the cup of salvation and call upon the name of the Lord* [Ps 115:13]. And also, in the Gospel: *Can you drink the cup that I am about to drink?* [Mt 20:22]. Also: *Taking the cup, he gave thanks* [Mt 26:27]. The gold chalice also signifies the treasury of wisdom hidden in Christ; the silver one, the purification of faults; the tin one, the resemblance between faults and punishments. Tin also stands between silver and lead, and clearly the Body of Christ was not made of lead, that is, from a sinful woman, but was nonetheless from a body that was similar to that of a woman born in sin; and it was not made of silver, that is a perishable body on account of her fault, but nonetheless was perishable on account of our faults, because: *He bore our sufferings and carried our*

sorrows [Isa 53:4]. More is said about the chalice and the paten under the heading *On consecrations and unctions*.[49]

46. But, anyone might say, out of contempt towards religion, that the Lord decreed to Moses that all of the vessels of the Tabernacle and everything used for the ceremonies had to be made of bronze, as stated in Exodus, chapters 27 and 28, and that precious vessels and ornaments and things of this sort could have been sold and given to the poor, which is similar to what Judas said to the women anointing the Lord. But we do this not because the Lord does not love cheap ornaments as much as those made of gold, but because men freely offer to God what they love the most, and they conquer their avarice by putting them in divine service. Besides, these things are our moral duty in service of divine piety and signify our future glory. And so in the Old Law it was decreed that the Priest's upper garments be made of gold, hyacinth, purple, twice-dyed scarlet, twisted flax, and other precious materials, to show with what diverse virtues the priest ought to shine; and the altar, the table of offering, the candelabra, and all of the other vessels and ornaments had to be made of gold or silver, as in Exodus chapters 25, 30, and 38. It was also decreed that the Tabernacle be made of diverse precious materials, as stated under the heading *On the Church*.[50] The priest of the Old Law used many other precious ornaments, as stated in the third part, under the heading *On the vestments of the Old Law*.[51] This topic is also discussed under the heading *On the dedication of a church*, near the beginning.[52]

47. Furthermore, it was prohibited by the Council of Orléans,[53] that the vessels of the divine mysteries be used for weddings, lest they be polluted by contact with the shameful things or the ceremonies of this world; through which is undoubtedly shown that no one should make a chasuble from the clothes of any given person, or to make from them ornaments destined for other divine mysteries.

48. Again, Pope Stephen[54] decreed that ecclesiastical vestments can not be put to other uses, nor can they even be touched unless by consecrated men [or clergy], lest the vengeance that struck Belshazzar,[55] the king of Babylon, befall those who transgress this decree.

49. Pope Clement[56] also decreed that the dead shall not be buried or wrapped or covered, nor shall their bier be covered with the pall [*palla*], that is, the altar cloths, or with the cloth [*mappa*] that covers the chalice, or with the cloth that the priest uses to clean his hands after the consecration.

50. When the palls, that is, the corporals [*corporalia*], and the veils, that is, the ornaments of the altar, or the coverings hanging on the altar become dirty, the deacons along with the lower orders of ministers will wash them in the sacristy, and not outside of it. And for washing the veils that service the cult of the altar, they will use a new basin; the palls, that is, the corporals, will be washed in another basin; the veils of the doorways, that is, the curtains that hang in church on feast days and during Lent are washed in another basin. Hence it was decreed by the Council of Lérida,[57] that there be proper vessels for no other use than washing the corporal and the altar coverings, in which nothing else ought to be washed. But according to the same Clement,[58] if the palls, that is, the vestments of the altar, or the chair covered with sacred vestments in which the priest sits, or the candelabrum, or the veil, that is, altar cloth [*pannus*], or the curtains hanging over the altar are consumed by old age, they shall be burned, and their ashes shall be cast in the baptistery, or into the walls, or into the cracks of the pavement where no one will pass. And note that the ecclesiastical ornaments are blessed, as discussed under the heading *On consecrations and unctions.*[59]

{ 4 }

ON THE BELLS

1. Bells [*campanae*] are bronze vessels first invented in Nola, a city in Campania; therefore the larger of these are called "campanae," from the region of Campania, while the smaller ones are called "nolae," from the city of Nola.

2. The church bell is rung and blessed so that through its effect and sound, the faithful are summoned, one after the other, to the eternal prize, and the devotion to their faith increases in them; also that the crops, minds, and bodies of those same believers are preserved; that hostile armies and all wicked enemies be repelled far away from us; that great clashes, wind storms, violent tempests, and lightening storms be restrained; that hostile thunderstorms and blazing winds be checked; that the spirits of rage and the powers of the air be prostrated; and, that those hearing the bell shall flee to the bosom of holy mother Church, falling before the standard [*vexillum*] of the holy cross, *before which every knee will bend*, etc. [Phil 2:10]; each of these reasons is given in the blessing of the bells.

3. It should also be noted that the bells, through whose sound the people come to church to hear and the clergy to announce the mercy of the Lord in the morning and His power at night [cf. Ps 91:3], signify the silver trumpets with which in the Old Law, the people were called for the sacrifice, which is discussed in the sixth part, under the heading *On Pentecost*.[1] And, just as the watchmen awaken the camp with trumpets, so too the ministers of churches arouse themselves with the sound of bells, so that they can pass the night against the snares of the Devil. But our bronze signals are more sonorous than the trumpets of the Old Law, because then, God was only known in Judea; now, He is known in the whole world. Ours are also more durable: they signify that the preaching

of the New Testament will be more durable than the trumpets and sacrifices of the Old Law, since it will last until the end of the world.

4. Indeed, the bells signify the preachers who ought to call the faithful to the faith, in the manner of bells, which was signified in what the Lord decreed to Moses: that he make a vestment for the High Priest having seventy-two bells that would ring when the Priest entered the Holy of Holies. The vase-shaped interior of the bell therefore represents the mouth of the preacher, according to the Apostle: *I have become as sounding brass or a ringing cymbal* [1 Cor 13:1].

5. The hardness of the metal designates the strength in the mind of the preacher, for which reason the Lord says: *I will give you a face harder than their faces* [Ezek 3:8]. The plectrum, or the rod of iron inside which strikes either side of the bell producing its sound, represents the tongue of the teacher, who is furnished with learning, and who can make each Testament resound.

6. A prelate without the education for preaching is like a bell without a plectrum, just as Gregory says: "A priest, if he is unlearned in preaching: what sort of cry shall he make, whose speech is silent, and who is like a dumb dog too feeble to bark?"[2] The striking of the plectrum denotes that the preacher must first strike the vices within himself, correcting himself, and afterwards go out to others and begin to reproach them, lest, contrary to the teaching of the Apostle, preaching to others, he himself is found to be blameworthy. And so the Psalmist says: *God said to the sinner: Why do you explain my statutes and profess my covenant with your mouth?* [Ps 49:16]. Through the example of his own passion for what he preaches, he inflames many others whom he cannot move by the skill of his speech. The chain by which the plectrum is attached or bound to the inside of the bell is the moderation which tempers the tongue of the preacher, which means to speak from the heart, that is, on the authority of Scripture, which is what moves the tongue of the preacher.

7. The wood from which the bell hangs signifies the wood of the Lord's cross; this is why the bell is sometimes kept in the highest place, because the cross was announced by the most ancient fathers. The implements, with which this wood is bound or attached, are the oracles of the Prophets; the iron ligature, which joins the bell to the wood, denotes the charity through which the preacher glories, as he is indissolubly bound to the cross, saying: *Be it far from me to glory, unless in the cross of our Lord Jesus Christ* [Gal 6:14]. The semicircular binding attached to the wood, in the middle of the top of the bell, by which it is rung, signi-

fies the virtuous mind of the preacher; attaching itself to the divine commandments, his preaching fills the ears of the faithful through frequent ringing.

8. The rope, which hangs down from the bell, with which it is rung, is the humility or the life of the preacher; the rope also represents the measure of our own life. Besides, since the rope is measured from the wood to where it meets the bell—the wood that is understood to mean the Lord's cross—the rope rightly designates sacred Scripture, which descends in a straight line from the holy cross. Just as the rope is made with three small strands, so too Scripture consists of three senses, namely: the historical, allegorical, and moral senses; the rope descending from the wood into the hand of the priest is Scripture descending from the mystery of the cross into the mouth of the preacher. And thus, the rope extends even beyond the hand of the one holding it because Scripture should pass into the works of the preacher. The rising and falling of the rope, when the bell is rung, denotes that sacred Scripture sometimes speaks of lofty things, sometimes of mundane things; or that sometimes the preacher says lofty things for some hearers and for others, condescends, according to what the Apostle says: *If we went to the heights it was for God; when we condescended, it was on account of you* [2 Cor 5:13].[3] And thus, the priest pulls the rope downward, so to speak, when he descends from the contemplative to the active life; and he himself is pulled upward when teaching the Scriptures, when he is elevated to contemplation. He pulls the rope downward when he understands the Scripture according to the letter (which kills); he is pulled upward when he explicates Scripture spiritually. And so according to Gregory,[4] the priest is pulled downward or upward when he measures these things in himself, namely, when he throws himself into sinful things or when he progresses in doing good works.

And when the bell rings with the pulling of the rope, the people are united for the exposition of sacred Scripture; the preacher is heard; the people are unified with the unity of faith and charity. Moreover, the priest, who recognizes that he is obligated to preach, does not retreat from using bells, since the sons of Aaron used to make a din with trumpets [cf. Num 10:8]. Thus he pulls the rope, who calls his brothers or the people with this ministry. The ring attached to the end of the rope, by which the rope is pulled in many different regions, is the crown or prize of perseverance to the end, or it is divine Scripture itself. Moreover, Pope Sabinian[5] decreed that the bells be rung by churches every hour of the day.

9. And note that for the Divine Offices, the bells are commonly rung twelve times for the twelve hours of the day, namely: once at Prime and similarly, once at the last hour, because all things come from one God, and He shall always be one and in all things. At Terce, they are rung three times, for the second, third, and fourth hours, which are then sung at this one hour. Similarly at Sext, they are thrice rung, for the three hours, namely: the fifth, sixth, and seventh hours. Similarly at None, for the three hours. At Vespers, which is the eleventh hour, they are not rung just once, but many times, since in the time of grace the preaching of the Apostles was multiplied. Also, they are often rung at night and in the morning, because it must often be exclaimed: *Arise, you who sleep, and rise up from among the dead* [Eph 5:14].

10. Generally, the bells are rung three times in the Night Office [*in nocturnis*]. First, with a handbell [*squilla*], which signifies Paul sagaciously preaching; the second ringing signifies Barnabas, who associated himself with him; the third indicates that when the Jews rejected the word of God, the Apostles turned themselves towards the Gentiles, to whom they gave faith in the Trinity, imbued with the teachings of four Gospels; and so in some places they ring the bells four times.

11. And note that there are six types of bells that are rung in church, namely: the handbell [*squilla*], the cymbal [*cymbalum*], the "nola" [*nola*], the "little nola" [*nolula*] or the double bell, and the large bell [*signum*]. The handbell is rung in the dining room, that is, in the refectory; the cymbal is rung in the cloister; the "nola" in the choir; the "little nola" or the double bell in the clock; the bronze bell [*campana*] in the bell tower; the large bell [*signum*], in the tower. For this reason, each of the hours can generally be named after the sort of bell rung. And the bells are assigned different names, since the preachers which they represent are engaged in many different tasks.

12. It is fitting, that during all of Septuagesima,[6] during which time Lent falls, on working feast days,[7] the bells should not be rung repeatedly, or vigorously, or from top to bottom, but only with a tinkling sound; that is, simply rung at each of the hours of the day or at Matins. Still, in churches that are well regulated, they are rung twice at Prime: first to call the community, second to begin the Office. At Terce, they are thrice rung, in accordance with the number of hours at this Office, as was said before: one, to call the community; one to gather them; the other to begin the Office. It is the same with Sext and None, and the same bells are simply rung in the same order as at Matins. At Mass and at Vespers two bells are always rung. In smaller churches, they should be rung sim-

ply, as noted above; and this is done on holidays. On the other hand, they are rung vigorously on Sundays and solemnities, as during other times. Since the preachers, who are represented by the bells, are more abundant in the time of grace, and they press on in convenient and inconvenient times, therefore, on feasts that pertain to grace, the bells are vigorously rung, and for a longer time than usual so that those who are sleeping or are in a drunken state are aroused, lest they oversleep. What the ringing symbolizes when the *Te Deum laudamus* is sung is discussed in the fifth part, under the heading *On the Night Office*.[8]

13. Also, when someone dies, the bells should be rung so that when the people hear this, they will pray for him. If it is a woman, some ring it twice, because she brought alienation into the world, because she first caused man to be alienated from God, which is why from that day she did not possess God's blessing. For a man it is rung three times, since the Trinity was found in a man; first Adam was formed from the earth, then woman from Adam, and afterwards man was created from both of them [cf. Gen 2:22; 4:1]; and thus we have a trinity. And if it is a cleric, it is simply rung as many times as he had orders.[9] Finally, all of the bells must be loudly rung so that the people know for whom they must pray; they must be loudly rung when the body is carried to the church and when it is carried from the church to the burial place.

14. Also, the bells are rung in processions so that the demons who fear them will flee, as discussed in the fourth part, under the heading, *On the accession of the pontiff to the altar*.[10] They are so fearful when they hear the trumpets of the Church militant, that is, the bells, that they are like some tyrant who is fearful when he hears in his own country the trumpets of some powerful king who is his enemy.

15. And this is why a church, seeing a violent storm arising, rings the bells, so that the demons, hearing the trumpets of the eternal King, that is, the bells, are terrified and flee, and they silence the storm; and this is why the faithful, when the bells are rung, are admonished and called on to stand firm and pray for the imminent danger. And the bells are silent during the three days before Easter, as discussed in the sixth part, under the heading *The fifth day, Holy Thursday*.[11] Also, during a time of interdict,[12] the bells are silent because often on account of the crime of those under interdict, the tongue of the preachers is obstructed, according to what the Prophet says: *I will make your tongue stick to your palate because this house*—that is, the people—*is rebellious*—that is, disobedient [Ezek 3:26]. The church also has an organ, about which we will speak in the fourth part, under the heading *On the Sanctus*.[13]

{5}

ON THE CEMETERY AND OTHER SACRED AND
RELIGIOUS PLACES

1. Now we shall speak about the cemetery and other sacred or religious places.[1] Some venerable places are fittingly designed out of human necessity, while others are dedicated to prayer. Places arising from human necessity are a hostel, a hospital (which is the same thing), a pharmacy, an elder hostel, an orphanage, and a place for wounded soldiers. For the holy fathers and the religious rulers established places of this sort in which the poor, the pilgrims, the old, orphans, infants, hermits, the sick, the feeble, and the wounded could be received and cared for. And note that the Greek word *ieronta* is translated *senex* [old man] in Latin.

2. Among those aforementioned places of prayer, some are sacred [*sacra*], some are holy [*sancta*], and some are religious [*religiosa*]. Those that are sacred have been dedicated in a ceremony by the hands of a bishop, and are sanctified by God; and these have various names, as previously noted under the heading *On the church building*.[2] Holy places are those that have immunity or privileges, and they are assigned to the servants and ministers of churches; places which, lest anyone presume to violate them, or seek a legal remedy or special privilege to violate them, carry the threat of certain punishment.[3] Among these places is the atrium of churches, and in some regions cloisters, within which are the dwellings of the canons; in these places, anyone fleeing from a crime, if he is received there,[4] is given protection, following the legal statutes governing the gates and theaters of cities.[5]

3. Religious places are those where an intact human cadaver, or at least a head is buried; since no one can have two sepulchers, a body or any other of its members buried without the head does not constitute a religious place. According to the legal statutes,[6] the cadaver of a Jew or

pagan or an unbaptized infant makes the place in which it is buried a religious place; but according to Christian teaching and canonical authority, only a Christian cadaver can make a place religious.[7] And note that any place that is sacred is also religious, but not the opposite. Moreover, this religious locus is called a variety of names, namely: a cemetery, or *poliantrum* or *andropolis*—"a city of man"—which it is. Also, a sepulcher, a mausoleum, which it in fact is; a dormitory [*dormitorium*], a burial mound [*tumulus*], a monument, a prison [*ergastulum*], a sarcophagus, a pyramid, a tomb for burning and burying [*bustum*], an urn, and a cave.

4. The word cemetery comes from *cymen*, which means "sweet," and *sterion*, which means, "abode," and there the bones of the dead sweetly find their repose and await the coming of the Savior. Or, because that is where there are bugs, that is, vermin that stink beyond measure.

5. A common graveyard [*poliantrum*] is so called as if to say, "defiled grotto" [*pollutum antrum*], on account of the cadavers of the men buried there. Or *poliantrum* is translated, "a multitude of men," from *polis*, which means "a multitude," and *andron*, which means "man"; and it follows that this is the proper meaning of cemetery, since a multitude of men is buried there. So too with *andropolis*, which means the same thing.

6. The word sepulcher can be taken to mean, "without a pulse," [*sine pulsu*] since the one buried there lacks a pulse, or because this is the place where bones are buried.

7. Mausoleum gets its name form a certain man who was called Mausoleus, who was a powerful man who was greatly loved by his wife, Artemesia; when he died, she built him a glorious sepulcher that she called a Mausoleum, after the name of her husband. And from that point the custom evolved that any costly sepulcher be called a mausoleum.[8]

8. Dormitory comes from the word "sleeping" [*dormiendo*], because in that place, the bodies of the saints, who are sleeping in the Lord, find their repose. Something is called a burial mound [*tumulus*], as if to say "swollen ground," [*tummens tellus*] because when a man is buried in the ground a small amount of dirt remains elevated above him.[9] It is called a monument, because it admonishes the mind [*monet mentem*] of anyone looking at it to remember that he is dust, and unto dust he shall return.[10] The word prison [*ergastulum*] comes from *arge*, which means "work," or from *erga*, which means "labor," and *sterion*, which means "station";[11] hence the bodies of those who have died in the Lord find

their repose there: *Blessed are those dead who died in the Lord hence-forth, and the Spirit says*, etc. [Rev 14:13].

9. Sarcophagus comes from the word *sarcos*, which means, "flesh," and *phagin*, which means, "to eat," because in it, the flesh is eaten and consumed.[12] Pyramid comes from *pir*, which means "fire," since cre-mated or incinerated bodies used to be kept there, or because the fire begins by burning a wide span and then it reaches a high point, just like a pyramid, and this is the highest sort of sepulcher.[13] This sort of thing was done in Rome, where the ashes of Julius Caesar were placed, but through a corruption of the word, it was commonly called the "needle of St. Peter," when it should have been called "Julian."[14] Caesar also made a pyramid near Tours, near the banks of the Loire River, and he enclosed there the ashes of a certain soldier who was his friend who had been killed.[15]

10. A tomb for burning and burying [*bustum*] derives its name from its contents, that is, a place in which burned remains or human bodies used to be buried. Something is called an urn from the ancient custom where human bodies were burned on a pyre and the ashes were gath-ered and placed in earthen urns and preserved. A cave [*spelunca*] is sometimes called "duplex," as we shall now show.

11. The cemetery is said to have originated with Abraham, who bought a field near Hebron, in which there were two caves where he was buried with Sarah, Isaac and Jacob, Adam and Eve; and he bought it to have a burial place for himself and his loved ones. There were two caves there so that two could be buried next to each other, namely, husband and wife, or in one, women and in the other men; or that this double cave was made in the form of a chair, so that each one could be buried there; and so Jerome[16] says that the three Patriarchs were buried in the city of Hebron, in double caves with their three wives. And they were buried as if they were sitting up, and the upper part of the cave, which housed the trunk of the body from its buttocks to its top, was called one cave, while the lower part which housed the feet, legs, and upper thighs, was called another cave.

12. Not everyone should be indiscriminately buried inside a church, for it seems that the place of burial is of no benefit.[17] Lucifer was thrown down from the heavens [cf. Isa 14:12; Apoc. 12:7–9] and Adam was ex-pelled from paradise [cf. Gen 3:24], and which of these places is better? Likewise, Joab was killed in his tabernacle [cf. 1 Chr 2:34], and Job tri-umphed in his dung heap. Indeed, it seems dangerous to bury an un-worthy or sinful person in a church. We read in the *Dialogues*[18] of Saint

Gregory, book 4, chapter 56, that when a certain infamous person was buried in the church of Blessed Faustinus of Brescia, that very night, Blessed Faustinus appeared to the custodian of that church, saying: "Tell the bishop to throw out the stinking flesh that he placed here; otherwise he will be dead in thirty days." The custodian was too frightened to tell this to the bishop, and on the thirtieth day, the bishop suddenly died.

We also read in the same book, chapter 57,[19] about another man who was buried in a church; that his cadaver was later found outside of the church and his coverings remained in the church; and Augustine[20] says: "Those who are weighed down by more serious sins, if they have themselves buried in a sacred place and remain there, shall be judged for their presumption, since the sacred places do not free them, but the defect of their recklessness shall accuse them." No body should ever be buried in church, near the altar, where the Body and Blood of the Lord are confected, unless they are the bodies of holy fathers whom we call patrons, that is, the defenders of the church, who by their merits, defend the entire region; and the bishops, abbots, holy priests, or laity of the greatest sanctity have a church burial, but all of them should be buried around the church, as in the atrium, or in the portico, or in the hallway, or the vaults attached to the exterior of the church, or in the cemetery. Some say that there should be a space of thirty feet around the entire church specifically consecrated for this purpose; others say that the course that the bishop follows around the church when he consecrates it suffices for this purpose. Augustine says, in his *Book on the Care of the Dead*,[21] near the end: "To be buried among the memorials erected to the Martyrs is profitable for the dead person, so that in entrusting him to the patronage of the Martyrs, the benefits of prayers for him will be increased."

13. In ancient times men could only be buried in their own homes, but, because of the stench of the cadavers, it was decreed that they be buried outside of the city; and they assigned a certain common place for this that was sanctified. The nobles used to be buried on mountains, and in the middle of mountains, or at their base and on their own estates. And if someone is killed in a siege, and cannot be put in a cemetery, he is buried wherever he could be put. If a merchant or pilgrim died at sea and there is land nearby, he is buried there; if the port city is far away, he is buried on a nearby island. If they cannot see land, they make a little wooden house for him, if they can, and toss him into the sea.

14. Only a baptized Christian ought to be buried in a Christian cemetery; nonetheless, not every Christian can be, since no one killed committing a crime—if the crime should be a mortal sin, such as in the case

of one killed in the act of adultery, or in theft, or in pagan games—can be buried there. Therefore, when there is doubt as to the cause of death, a man should be buried wherever he is found. If he suddenly dies playing customary games, such as a sporting game, he can be buried in the cemetery, since nobody intended to kill him. But since he was occupied with mundane things, some say that he must be buried without Psalms and without other funeral rites. And if anyone incites another into a brawl or violent disturbance, and he dies unconfessed, and he did not ask for a priest, he should not, as some say, be buried in a cemetery; nor should anyone who caused his own death by his own hands; an exception is if he died fighting in defense of those under his care or his household, and he remained penitent as he died. If for no apparent reason, but only through the judgment of God, someone suddenly dies, he can be buried in the cemetery. For the just man is saved, in whatever hour he dies, especially if he was engaged in any sort of legitimate work. The defenders of justice and those killed in a just war are freely granted the cemetery and the Divine Offices, but the dead should not be carried into the church, lest its pavement be polluted with their blood. But if anyone is returning from a brothel, or from any other place where he might have fornicated, and he is killed en route, or he dies for some unknown cause, he is not to be buried in a common cemetery; and this is the case if it can be proven that he fornicated, and if it is not established that afterwards he confessed and was contrite; otherwise, he can receive a proper burial.

15. Again, according to some, a woman dying in childbirth should not be placed in a church, lest, as some say, the pavement of the church be polluted with her blood; her funeral should be held outside the church, and she should be buried in the cemetery. But this does not seem right, since her suffering is turned into a fault on her part. For this reason it is permissible for her to be carried into church, so long as the church, lest it be polluted, is carefully guarded from the stains of her body.

16. Nevertheless, the stillborn child, extracted dead from her womb, not having been baptized, is buried outside of the cemetery. Yet there are some who say that the stillborn child ought to be buried with its mother within the cemetery, since it may be counted among the mother's entrails.[22]

17. Fittingly, a man and his wife can be buried in the same sepulcher, following the example of Abraham and Sarah, who did not choose a specific sepulcher; and so Tobias ordered his son, that when his mother had filled out her days, he place her with him in the same sepulcher [cf.

Tob 14:12]. Also, anyone should be buried in the sepulcher of his parents, unless, because of piety, he has chosen to be buried elsewhere. Furthermore, at the Council of Mainz,[23] it was decreed that those who are hanged, and who on account of their sins have been given the greatest penalty, may, if they have confessed or have desired to confess and have received communion, be buried in a cemetery and prayers and Masses can be offered for them. How a human body should be buried will be discussed in the seventh part, under the heading *On the Office of the Dead.*[24]

{6}

ON THE DEDICATION OF A CHURCH

Since, in previous chapters, mention has already been made of the church and the altar, it follows that we should add other things concerning their dedication, discussing first, where the consecration of a church originated; second, by whom it is consecrated; third, why; fourth, how a church should be dedicated and what the dedication and each of its individual details signifies. In the seventh part, the Office for the Feast of the Dedication of a Church will be discussed.[1]

1. First, it should be stated where the dedication of a church originated, about which it should be noted that Moses, following the Lord's precept, made a Temple and consecrated it with a table and an altar, as well as bronze utensils for the celebration of the divine cult; and not only did he consecrate them with prayers to God, he also smeared them with holy oil, following the command of the Lord. For we read that the Lord commanded Moses to make a chrism with which he should anoint the Tabernacle and the Ark of the Testament on the day of their dedication [cf. Ex 20:36]. Solomon, the son of David, following the Lord's command, also made a Temple with an altar, and consecrated it and everything else that was used for the divine cult, just as we find in the Book of Kings [cf. 1 Chr 6]. Also, King Nebuchadnezzar convened all of the satraps, nobles, and tyrants for the dedication of a gold statue that he had made. And the Jews, as we read in Burchard, book 3, in the chapter, *The Jews*,[2] had consecrated with sacred prayers the places where they used to offer sacrifices to God, and they made no offerings to the Lord in any place except in the ones that had been dedicated to God. If those who zealously served in the shadow of the Law used to do this, how much

more should we—to whom the Truth has been clearly revealed, and to whom grace and truth have been given through Jesus Christ—build a temple for the Lord and furnish it as well as we are able, and to consecrate it devoutly and solemnly with sacred prayers, holy unctions, as well as with altars, vessels, vestments, and the other things that pertain to the divine cult, following the instruction of Pope Felix III.[3]

In the city of Beirut, in Syria, when the Jews had defiled a certain image of the crucifix with their feet, and they pierced its side, blood and water immediately flowed from it. And seeing this, the Jews were amazed, and the sick among them, when smeared with this blood, were freed from all of their illnesses; on this account, all of them, receiving faith in Christ, were baptized and they consecrated all of their synagogues, making them churches. Thus the custom arose that churches should be consecrated, when before, only altars had been consecrated. And on account of this miracle, the church decreed that a commemoration of the Lord's Passion be celebrated the fifth day before the calends of December, and in Rome a church was consecrated in honor of the Savior where a vial with that blood is preserved and a solemn feast is celebrated for that event.[4]

2. Second, it should be noted that only a bishop can dedicate churches and altars, since he bears the image and figure of the High Priest, that is, Christ, who is spiritually dedicating them, without whom we cannot establish anything in grace; for which reason He says: *Without me you can do nothing* [Jn 15:5], and the Psalmist: *Unless the Lord builds the house* [Ps 126:1]. Thus the Council of Carthage prohibits[5] a priest from doing these things, nor can anyone in lower orders be asked to do this.

3. A church, as the sacred canons fittingly teach, must not be dedicated until it is endowed, and from legitimate means. For we read[6] that when a certain bishop consecrated a church that had been constructed from usury and theft, he saw the Devil behind the altar, resting in the bishop's chair, dressed in pontifical vestments; and he said to the bishop: "Stop consecrating this church; it is under my jurisdiction, since it was built from usury and theft." The bishop and the clergy were terrified, and when they were fleeing, the Devil immediately destroyed the church with a great din.

4. Furthermore, a church in which an infidel or pagan is buried, or where there is the accusation of avarice, should not be consecrated until the cadaver has been expelled from there, and the church, when the walls and beams have been cleansed, is reconciled; and the same thing

is done if an excommunicate is there.[7] If a pregnant woman is buried there, it can be consecrated without removing her, even if her fetus is not baptized, even though certain learned men have written otherwise.[8] And a church can be consecrated on Sundays and on ordinary days, and by many bishops, and many altars can be consecrated at the same time by one bishop in the same church.[9]

5. Third, we must state why a church is dedicated, and there are five reasons. First, so that the Devil and his power can be entirely driven out; for this reason Gregory reports in his *Dialogues*,[10] book 3, chapter 30, that when a certain church that had belonged to the Arians was restored to the faithful and was being reconsecrated, and the relics of Saint Sebastian and Blessed Agatha had been transferred there, the people who had gathered there suddenly felt a pig running here and there between their feet, which once outside of the church, no one could see; and this filled everyone with amazement. Thus the Lord first indicated that he would disclose to all that the unclean inhabitant of that place would leave. The following night, there was a huge noise on the roof of that church, as if someone were running upon it, and on the second night, an even louder sound erupted there; and on the third night, such a loud noise was heard, it seemed as if the entire church would be turned upside down, and then immediately the noise began to die down, and afterwards, the ancient enemy never again appeared to trouble that place. Secondly, a church is dedicated so that anyone fleeing to it can be saved, as we read in the canon of Gregory;[11] this is why Joab fled into the Tabernacle and grabbed the horns of the altar [cf. 2 Chr 8]. Third, so that prayers offered there might be heard, thus in the prayer at Mass it says: "Grant that all who are assembled here to pray, in whatever tribulation they have, may receive the benefits of Your consolation."[12] So too did Solomon pray in the dedication of the Temple, as we read in 3 Kings, chapter 8 [cf. 2 Chr 8]. Fourth, so that our prayers can be offered to God there, as was stated under the heading, *On the church*.[13] Fifth, so that the ecclesiastical sacraments can be administered, for which reason the church itself is called a "tabernacle," as if to say it is "God's inn" [*taberna Dei*] in which the divine sacraments are housed and administered.

6. Fourth, we must state how a church is consecrated.[14] First, when everyone is removed from the church, with only the deacon remaining inside, the bishop with the clergy standing in front of the doors, blesses the salted water; meanwhile, inside the church, twelve lamps burn before the twelve crosses depicted on the walls of the church. Afterwards,

the clergy, with the people following, walk around the exterior of the church three times, and with a bunch of hyssop branches, they asperse the walls with the blessed water; and any time he arrives in front of the doors of the church, the bishop strikes the lintel with his pastoral staff, saying: "Lift up your doors, Θ princes," etc., and then the deacon responds: "Who is this King of Glory?" to which the bishop replies: "Our mighty Lord," etc. On the third time around, with the door open, the bishop enters the church with a few of his ministers, and with the clergy and the people remaining outside, he says: "Peace to this house," and then he recites the litanies. He then makes a cross out of ashes and sand on the pavement of the church, where all of the Greek and Latin letters of the alphabet are written. The bishop then blesses more water with salt and ashes and wine, and consecrates the altar. He then anoints with holy chrism the twelve crosses on the church walls.

7. Truly, whatever is done here visibly, God accomplishes in the soul through an invisible power, which is the true temple of God, where faith establishes the foundation, hope builds it up, and charity perfects it. For the Catholic Church itself, made into one out of many living stones, is the temple of God; though there are many temples, there is only one temple that has only one God and one faith. The house must be dedicated; the soul must be sanctified.

8. And it should be noted that the consecration of a church has two effects: it appropriates the material church and us to God, implying the betrothal to God of the Church and the soul of any of the faithful. A house that is not consecrated is like a girl destined for some man, but not yet dowered, nor with a marriage contract for a carnal union. But in the consecration, she is given a dowry and passes over to her true spouse, Jesus Christ; and it is a sacrilege afterwards to violate her through adultery. For the house ceases to be the brothel of demons, as is clearly shown in the consecration of that temple that used to be called the Pantheon.[15]

9. First, then, we must discuss the holy water, about which the Lord said: *Unless you shall be born again by water and the Holy Spirit, you shall not enter in the Kingdom of heaven* [Jn 3:5]. For water, which is suitable for washing the body, is worthy to receive divine power, for just as it cleanses the body of filth, so too does it cleanse souls from their sins. It is clear, then, that this water, by whose aspersion the church is consecrated, signifies Baptism, since in a certain manner, the church itself is baptized. Indeed, that same church certainly represents *the* Church that

is contained in it, namely, the multitude of the faithful, and so it too receives its name "church"—containing one, plainly, for each of its contents.

10. It should be asked, moreover, why salt must be mixed with this water, since our Savior never made any mention of salt when speaking of Baptism. He did not say: "Unless you shall be born again from salt water, or water mixed with salt," or something else of this sort, but he said: *Unless you shall be born again from water and the Holy Spirit*, etc. [Jn 3:5]. The same thing can be asked about the oil and the chrism. But it should be noted that in sacred speech salt is often a symbol of wisdom, according to what is written: *May your speech be seasoned with salt* [Col 4:6]. And the Lord said to his disciples: *Have salt in yourselves, and be at peace among yourselves* [Mk 9:49]. And also: *You are the salt of the earth, but if salt becomes tasteless, with what shall it be seasoned?* [Mt 5:13]. For this reason, according to the Law, no holocaust was offered without salt, and it was used in every sacrifice, by which one may be convinced that salt represents wisdom. And wisdom is the seasoning for all of the virtues just as salt is for all foods. And this is why no one can be baptized without first consuming salt; even infants, who, though they cannot participate in the act, can have salt as a symbol of the sacrament; nor can the water be blessed without salt. We will speak about other blessings with water in the following treatise.[16]

11. The triple aspersion with hyssop of both the inside and outside of the church signifies the triple immersion in a Baptism. And this is done for three reasons. First, for the expulsion of demons, for the blessed water has the particular power to expel demons. Thus in the exorcism of the water it says: "That the water may be exorcized to put to flight all power of the enemy and to eradicate the enemy himself,"[17] etc. Second, for the purification and expiation of the church itself, for all earthly things are corrupted and soiled by sin. This is why in the Law everything used to be thoroughly cleansed with water. Third, to remove all curses and to introduce blessings to the place. For earth, from its beginning, received its curse from its own fruit, since by its own fruit was deception achieved; but water was never subjected to any curse.[18] This is why the Lord ate fish, but He is never expressly said to have eaten meat, unless He was eating the paschal lamb, and He did this on account of the precepts of the Law, thereby providing the example that sometimes it is permissible to abstain and sometimes to consume. Furthermore, the aspersion done around the outside of the church signifies that the Lord,

having concern for His own, sent His angel to surround those who fear Him [cf. Ps 33:8].

12. The three Responses that are sung while this happens are the joy of the three orders who received the faith, namely: Noah, Daniel, and Job. And because the grace of faith, hope, and charity is poured into this invocation, the base, the middle, and the highest part of the wall are sprinkled. The interior sprinkling will be discussed soon; the power of hyssop will be discussed in the following chapter.

13. The triple course that the bishop makes while aspersing the outside represents the triple course that Christ made for the sanctification of the Church. The first was that by which He came down from heaven into the world; the second was that by which He descended from earth into the underworld; the third, was that by which He returned from the underworld, and rising up from the dead, He ascended into heaven. The triple course also shows that a church is dedicated in honor of the Trinity. It shows too, the three orders of the saved in the Church: the virgins, the continent, and the married, which is also shown in the arrangement of the material church, as was stated under the heading on the church building.[19]

14. Furthermore, the triple knocking on the lintel of the door signifies the triple authority that Christ has in His Church, on account of which the door must be opened to Him: by right of His creation of it, its redemption, and the promise of its future glorification. For the bishop represents Christ, and his pastoral staff, Christ's power. Thus, the triple knocking on the door with the pastoral staff is understood to mean the preaching of the Gospel. What is a pastoral staff, except the word of God? And according to the saying of Isaiah, chapter 11: *He shall strike the earth with his staff*, that is, *with the word of his mouth* [Isa 11:4]. Thus, to strike the doors with the staff is to strike the ears of the audience with the voice of the preacher. The ears are the doors through which are brought the words of sacred preaching to the hearts of those hearing them, and so the Psalmist says: *You who have raised me up from the gates of death, that I might announce your praises in the gates of the daughters of Zion* [Ps 9:15]. What are the gates of the daughters of Zion except the ears and the hearing of the faithful? Third, the triple knocking with the staff and the opening of the doors signifies that through the preaching of the Church's pastors, the faithless come to fullness of the faith. Through this preaching, the doors of justice are opened, and those confessing the faith enter through them, for which reason the Psalmist

says: *Open the gates of justice for me, and entering them, I shall confess the Lord; this gateway is the Lord's and the just shall enter through it* [Ps 117:19–20]. The bishop therefore knocks on the lintel, that is with prayer, saying: "I entreat you, O princes," that is, the demons, or rather men, "to get up," that is, open "the doors," that is, remove the ignorance from your hearts.[20]

15. Indeed, the question of the deacon—"Who is this King of Glory?"— who is still concealed in the church, who responds on behalf of the people, is the ignorance of the same people who do not know who He is [Christ] who must enter.

16. The opening of the door is the emptying out of sin, for which reason the bishop fittingly knocks three times, because this number is well known and is most holy; and in every dedication the bishop must knock three times on the doors, because no sacrament can be performed in church without the invocation of the Trinity.

17. The triple proclamation: "Lift up the doors," etc., signifies the triple power of Christ, namely, that which He has in heaven, in the world, and in the underworld. Thus the hymn of the Ascension is sung: "That the threefold work of creation, of heavenly, earthly, and infernal things, being now subjected, bends its knee."[21]

18. Afterwards, with the door open, the bishop enters to denote that if he discharges the duties of his office, no one can resist him, according to the text: "O Lord, who can resist your power?"[22] He enters with two or three clerics, so that words of consecration remain in the mouth of two or three witnesses; or because the Lord, while he prayed for the Church, was transfigured in front of only a few who were present. And entering, the bishop says: "Peace to this house and to all who dwell here,"[23] because entering the world, Christ made peace between God and man. He came so that he could reconcile us to God the Father.

19. Afterwards, while the litanies are sung, the bishop prostrates himself and prays for the sanctification of this house. For Christ, humbled before his Passion, prayed for his disciples and all who would believe in Him, saying: *Father, make them holy in Your name* [Jn 17:11]. After he has risen up, the bishop prays without a salutation, since he does not say: "The Lord be with you," because, in a manner of speaking, the church is still unbaptized, and catechumens are not so worthy that they should be greeted this way, since they have not been sanctified; but we should still pray for them.

20. The clergy that are praying and chanting represent the Apostles who used to intercede to God for the sanctification of the Church and

her souls. The alphabet is written on the pavement of the church in the following manner: a cross of ashes and sand is made, which goes across the church, and upon this cross of dust are written the Greek and Latin letters of the alphabet, in the form of a cross; but not the Hebrew letters, since the Jews have withdrawn from the faith; and these letters are made with the pastoral staff.

21. The alphabet written on the cross represents three things. The first, as some say, is that writing the Greek and Latin letters of the alphabet in the shape of a cross represents the fellowship or union in faith of each people, namely, the Jews and the Gentiles, achieved through the cross of Christ, according to what is written: *Crossing his hands, Jacob blessed his sons* [Gen 48:14–15]. And this cross, which is drawn from one corner of the church to the other—namely, one section goes from the left corner in the eastern part to the right corner in the western part, and the other section goes from the right corner in the eastern part to the left corner in the western part—signifies that these people [the Jews], who were previously on the right, were moved to the left, and those who were at the head of the line were moved to the very back; and the ones on the left went right, and the ones in the back of the line went to its head, and this happened because of the power of the cross.[24] Coming from the east, Christ left the Jews on his left side, since they were faithless, and he came to the Gentiles, to whom, though they were in the west, He gave the right to be on his right-hand side; and at last, having placed the Gentiles on the right in the east, He shall visit the Jews in the left corner in the west, who remain inferior to the Gentiles to whom He first came. Thus, these letters are not written directly but at an angle, and in the form of a cross, since those who do not accept the mystery of the cross and who do not believe that they are saved by the Passion of Christ cannot fully reach this sacred knowledge. Wisdom will not enter a malevolent soul, and where Christ is not the foundation, nothing can be built.

22. Second, writing the alphabet represents the pages of both Testaments, which were fulfilled in the cross of Christ. For in His Passion, the veil of the Temple was torn in two, because the Scriptures were then revealed and the Holy of Holies was opened; and thus dying, He said: *It is finished* [Jn 19:30]. Indeed, in these few letters, all learning is contained, and the cross is drawn across the church from corner to corner because one Testament is contained in the other. It was a wheel inside of another wheel.

23. Third, it represents the articles of faith, since the pavement of the church is the foundation of our faith. The rudimentary letters written

there are the articles of faith with which the ignorant and the neophytes among either people in the church ought to be instructed; those who must count themselves as dust and ashes, according to what was said by Abraham, in Genesis chapter 18: *I will speak to my Lord though I am dust and ashes* [Gen 18:27]. The writing of the alphabet on the pavement is also the simple doctrine of the faith in the human heart.

24. The large cross or the pastoral staff, with which the alphabet is written, shows the teaching of the Apostles or the ministry of the Doctors of the Church, through which the conversion of the Gentiles took place and the faithlessness of the Jews was shown. The bishop then processes to the altar standing, and says: "O God, come to my assistance," and finally the first prayer of this Office begins.[25]

25. The verse, "Glory to the Father," etc., is recited since this blessing is done to display the glory of the Trinity; but nevertheless, "Alleluia" is not recited, for the reason given in the following chapter. And the bishop consecrates the altar, for which consecration more water is blessed—as will be discussed in the next chapter—with which he sprinkles the altar seven times. He sprinkles the interior of the entire church three times, just as he did outside, making no distinction between larger or smaller stones, since for God, there is no distinction among persons. Thus, the interior is sprinkled to denote that an external purification means nothing without an interior cleansing. Therefore, as previously noted, it is sprinkled three times; an aspersion that signifies the sprinkling and cleansing of Baptism which is given through the gift of the Trinity, according to what is written: *Go forth and teach all nations, baptizing them in the name of the Father, the Son and the Holy Spirit* [Mt 28: 19]. Since a church cannot be immersed in water as someone about to be baptized is immersed, the interior is sprinkled three times with water to replace triple immersion in water.

26. And water is sprinkled going from east to west, and one time in the middle of the church, in the form of a cross, since Christ decreed that all of Judea and all nations be baptized in the name of the Trinity; a Baptism to which He gave its efficacy through the ministry of His Passion, beginning with the Jews, among whom He was born. And the remaining water is poured out at the base of the altar, as will be discussed in the next chapter. Nevertheless, some ministers do not bless more water but complete the entire Office with the water that is already blessed. Meanwhile, the choir chants the Psalm: *Let God rise up and His enemies will be scattered* [Ps 67:2], and this one: *You who dwell in the shelter*, etc. [Ps 90:1], where mention is made of the church and its con-

secration, as it clearly says: *He who makes a dwelling in his house for the forsaken* [Ps 67:7]. The bishop then says: "My house shall be called a house of prayer,"[26] for his duty is to make the church a house of God, not a place of business.

27. Fittingly, the same chrism used for the altar is used for the anointing of the twelve crosses on the walls of the church. These crosses are painted, in the first place, to terrify the demons, so that when the demons that have been expelled from there see the sign of the cross, they will be terrified and not presume to return there. In the second place, they are signs of triumph, for the crosses are battle standards of Christ and the signs of His triumph. It is right, therefore, that crosses be painted there to show that this place is subjected to the dominion of Christ.

28. Now in imperial ceremonial, the practice is observed that in any city that hands itself over to an emperor, the imperial standard is set up there. And a certain likeness of this is shown figuratively in Genesis, chapter 28, where it says that Jacob set up as a monument the rock upon which he had laid his head, namely, as a sign of commendation, remembrance, and triumph [cf. Gen 28:10–22].

29. Third, so that they reflect on the Passion of Christ, by which He Himself consecrated His Church, and that faith in the Passion will be implanted in their memory, and so in Canticles it says: *Set me as a seal on your arm*, etc. [Song 8:6]. The twelve lamps placed in front of those crosses signify the twelve Apostles, who illuminated the entire world with their faith in the Crucified, and by whose teaching, the darkness was scattered, for which reason Blessed Bernard says: "All prophecy is verified by the faith of the Crucified."[27] And the Apostle: *For I judge myself to know nothing among you except Jesus Christ and Him crucified* [1 Cor 2:2]. Thus the crosses on the four walls are illuminated and anointed with chrism, since the Apostles, preaching the mystery of the cross, illuminated the four corners of the world with faith in the Passion of Christ; they enflamed them with knowledge, they anointed them with love, and the exercise of conscience, which is designated by the oil, and the odor of a good reputation, which is designated by the balm. Then, after the anointing of the altar, the altar and the church are decorated, the lamps are lit, and Mass is said, for which the pontiff uses vestments other than the ones he used for the aspersion rite, as will be discussed in the next chapter.

30. Finally, it must be noted that we say that a church is consecrated through the blood of someone; for which reason, according to Popes Pelagius and Nicholas,[28] the Roman Church was consecrated in the

martyrdom of the Apostles Peter and Paul. And so the church is consecrated, as previously discussed, and the altar, as noted in the following chapter, and the cemetery, and other things, as discussed under the heading *On consecrations.*[29]

31. And although we read in the Old Testament that the Temple was consecrated three times [cf. 1 Chr 8; 1 Ezra 6:14–22; 1 Macc 4:52–59]—first, in September; second, in March, under Darius; third, in December, under Judas Maccabaeus—a church is consecrated only once, and it should not be reconsecrated, unless by chance, it has been desecrated. This happens, first, if all of its walls have been badly burned, or if the greater part of the walls have been stripped by the fire, as noted in Leviticus, chapter 14, near the end [cf. Lev 14:49–57]. If only the roof or some part of it was destroyed by fire, and the walls remain standing, or only a small part of them was destroyed, the church is not reconsecrated.[30]

Second, if the whole church, or the greater part of it collapses all at once, and it is repaired from all or some of the stones that fell, mixed with other stones; for the consecration of a church consists, above all, in the anointing of the exterior, and in the joining and placement of the stones. If, on the other hand, the walls fell into ruin over time and were then repaired, it would still be counted as the same church and therefore ought not to be reconsecrated but only be reconciled with exorcised water and a solemn Mass,[31] even though some learned men have written that it should be reconsecrated.

Third, a church must be reconsecrated if it is doubtful that it was ever consecrated, and there is no text or picture or sculpture treating this event; and there is no evidence that anyone saw it, or heard about it, which, as some say, would suffice as testimony.[32]

32. Also, an altar that has been consecrated ought not to be reconsecrated unless it happens to be desecrated. This would happen first, if the table, that is, the upper part in which the consecration principally took place, is moved or seriously deformed, or it is badly broken, or cracked down the middle;[33] serious damage of this sort must be referred to the judgment of a bishop. It is an equally grave case if the entire structure of the altar has been moved or repaired. Nevertheless, a church ought not to be reconsecrated on account of the movement or damage of the structure of the altar, since the consecration of the altar is one thing, the consecration of the church another.[34] If the opposite happens, that is, the church is totally destroyed and the altar is not damaged, only the church is repaired and the altar is not reconsecrated; however, it is fitting to wash the altar with exorcized water.[35]

33. Even though the main altar has been consecrated, the other minor altars ought nonetheless to be consecrated, even though some might say it suffices to point to the minor altars during the consecration of the main altar.

34. If the altar has suffered a bit of damage on the corners, it should not on account of this be reconsecrated.[36] Second, an altar is reconsecrated if its seal—that is, the small stone that covers the cavity or hole in which the relics are stored, enclosed and sealed—has been moved or broken.[37] And this cavity sometimes is on the top part of the base of the altar; and sometimes another seal is not laid upon it, but the principal table, placed on top of the base, takes the place of the seal. Sometimes this cavity is in the back part of the altar, sometimes in the front; as evidence of the consecration, letters signed by the bishop—containing his name, the names of the other bishops who were present, the name of the Saint in whose honor it was consecrated, noting whether the church and altar were consecrated at the same time, the year and the date of the consecration—are carefully placed inside the cavity.

Third, the altar is reconsecrated if the joint which holds the seal to the cavity, or the table to the base or some other seal attached to it is broken; or if some of the stones joined to the base of the altar that touch the table or seal are moved or broken. For joining the seal to the cavity and the table to the base or lower structure are specifically understood to be the consecration itself.

Fourth, an altar is reconsecrated if an addition to the table or the lower structure has been made, and if this addition has changed the original form of the altar, since the form of something constitutes its being. A minor addition is not a profanation of it, since the sacred draws unto itself what is not sacred, as long as little has changed in the connection of the table to the lower structure.

Fifth, just as with a church, an altar is reconsecrated if it is doubtful that it was consecrated.[38]

Sixth,[39] some say that a portable altar [altare uiaticum] ought to be reconsecrated if the stone part is removed from the wood frame in which it is inserted, since it represents, in a manner of speaking, the seal; and whether it is put back in the same frame or not, it nonetheless ought to be reconsecrated; others affirm that it only needs to be reconciled. Since it is often carried from one place to another by order of the bishop, and carried along the road—for which reason it is called a "portable altar" or viaticum—it should not, on account of this movement, be reconsecrated or reconciled.

35. What if a consecrated chalice is gilded over: should it never be re-consecrated? For it seems to be a new chalice; it seems, too, the crafts-man has made a new work, since he has changed the original appear-ance of the work,[40] and that he who repairs the work reshapes it.[41] Indeed, the surface of a thing is what is consecrated, which is why I said before that a church must be reconsecrated if the walls have been damaged.

36. The opposite, however, is true since neither because of the white-washing or the painting of the walls, nor because of a minor addition ought the church to be reconsecrated, as I said before. It follows that if the form of the chalice has not been changed, the same chalice remains, which ought not to be reconsecrated, just as it was said before about a repaired church, because it remains the same; it would be otherwise if its prior form were changed into something entirely different, since the form of something constitutes its being, as I said. Nevertheless, it is proper to wash the chalice with exorcized water on account of its con-tact with dirty hands or with profane material, before it is used for the offering of the most holy Body and Blood of the Lord. Having spoken of consecrations, we shall now speak of reconciliation.[42]

37. On this subject, it should be noted that the spiritual temple, which is man, is sometimes polluted, as it says in Leviticus, chapter 15: *A man who suffers from a flow of semen shall be unclean* [Lev 15:2], and the same is true in a woman who is suffering from the flow of menstrual blood, or some other flow, as stated in the same text, in chapter 15 [cf. Lev 15:25–27]. And therefore, it is prohibited for the one who is polluted to enter the church until he is washed and purified with water, and Numbers, chapter 19, says that anyone who touches a cadaver is un-clean, so he is sprinkled with water and then shall be made clean [cf. Lev 19:11], and the Prophet says: *Cleanse me of my sin with hyssop, and I shall be clean* [Ps 50:9].

38. The material temple, which is the church, is itself polluted, ac-cording to the testimony of Pope Gregory,[43] and Leviticus, chapter 15; and so the Prophet says: *They have polluted Your holy temple* [Ps 78:1]. And today, the church is similarly washed with water and reconciled. The reconciliation is done with the celebration of a Mass, and with the sprinkling of solemnly blessed water, mixed with wine, salt, and ashes.[44] The salt clearly signifies discretion; the water, the people; the wine, di-vinity; the ashes, the Passion of Christ; the mixture of wine and water, the union of the Godhead and humanity. And these things are mixed to denote that the people, purified by the distinct memory of Christ's Pas-

sion, are joined to Christ Himself. This is done by a bishop, just as if it were the consecration of a church, although his coadjutor [*coepiscopus*] can also do the whole thing, that is, the blessing of the water and the reconciliation, or only the blessing of the water, or only the reconciliation, with the water that was previously blessed; but none of these things can be done by a simple priest, unless, by chance, he has the authority through the grant of a special privilege.

If a church is not consecrated, it should immediately be washed with exorcized water, following the decree of Gregory IX;[45] and some assert that this washing can be done, at the order of a bishop, by a simple priest, provided that he has exorcized water, which can be made by any priest. But some experts, of the most renowned authority, have written that the safest course of action is that as long as the bishop can do this, he should not entrust this to a simple priest; for the sacred canons[46] define "exorcized water" as solemnly blessed water mixed with wine and ashes; this is indeed true for the consecration of an unconsecrated church that is nevertheless dedicated to God.[47] It is otherwise, however, if it is a simple oratory, which is neither a sacred nor a religious place, which, as one might expect, someone establishes, as he desires, as a place to pray; but it cannot lawfully be used as a place to celebrate the liturgy without a diocesan license, nor can that place be assigned to some other use through the wish of the owner.[48] A church, however, must be reconciled in the case that follows.

39. First, if the place is polluted in flagrant or libidinous acts of sins—on account of adultery, if it is committed there, or because of fornication, and generally with anyone's seed emitted there: namely, with a married or unmarried woman; a cleric or layman; a heretic or a pagan; with natural or unnatural practices.[49] It is also polluted if a man has carnal knowledge of his own wife there, even though their sexual intercourse is legitimate and permissible in other places, this is not so at just any time or place.[50] And though many learned men think the contrary, we think it is a different case, if someone is polluted there while they are asleep; for them what should be lamented is what the soul has suffered, more than what the body has done;[51] as likewise the emission of semen there by any brute animal is not a sin, since reason is absent.[52]

40. A church ought to be reconciled when a homicide has taken place there, with or without bloodshed, in whatever manner it was deliberately done;[53] so also with any other sort of violence short of homicide that has taken place there that involves the shedding of human blood, either with or without a wound, from the nose or the mouth, since in

the Old Testament, Leviticus, chapters 13 and 15, both the shedding of human blood and the emission of semen were prohibited in the Temple, and both those who committed or suffered such things were not allowed to enter the Temple. But a church ought not to be reconciled if the bloodshed occurs without violence or injustice, that is, if the flow of blood is from the nose or mouth or a scar, or after a bleeding, or from hemorrhoids, or during menstruation, or from any other natural causes, or if someone is hurt there accidentally, or while playing. Nor is a church reconciled if an animal dies there, or if anybody suddenly dies there, or is killed by a falling rock or a beam, or is struck by lightning, or dies in similar sorts of circumstances. If someone who was mortally wounded outside takes refuge in the church, and after a great loss of blood, dies there, the church is not reconciled because the homicide was not actually committed in the church. If, on the other hand, he was wounded in church and then died outside, and the blood flowed from his wound outside the church, it is another matter; likewise if he bled only a little inside the church, since the blows that caused the wound are what matter.[54] If blood has been shed or human semen has been emitted on the roof of the church, it ought not to be reconciled, since these things occurred outside the church.

41. As for the rest, if a theft or a rape occurs in church, it is reconciled, according to the customs that apply to such cases. Some affirm that the same ought to be reconciled following the commission of whatever sort of violence, even though it might not involve bloodshed, since in the law, it is equal to fornication;[55] when, for example, someone fleeing there is carried out of the church through violent means,[56] or someone commits a burglary there, or if a violent brawl occurs without bloodshed, or if someone is violently beaten there with broken bones or bruises, but is not bleeding, or someone is presently condemned to death or mutilation and is dragged out and led to the place of execution.[57] But, since these cases or not expressly found in the law, it is not necessary for a bishop solemnly to reconcile the church; we think it can appropriately be washed by a priest with exorcized water, at the order of a bishop. It seems that the same ought to be said if a church, which for a long time has lacked a roof or doors, is by chance filled with manure and other filth from animals and the natural uses of men, such as lodging of some sort; nor would it be a bad thing in such a case to have it reconciled through the solemn blessing of a bishop.

If, however, anyone who was killed outside of the church is immediately brought into the church, and his murderer or someone else enters the church and does not think he is dead, and then inflicts a wound on the warm body from which blood flows, the church must be reconciled, as much for the horror and abomination, as for the violence and the willful sin; for even though the dead man is no longer strictly speaking a man, nevertheless, human blood has been spilled there by violence; for the violence, horror and injury have been inflicted on the cadaver itself.[58] The opposite is true if he dies naturally, and in preparing the corpse for a funeral and in his honor, he is dismembered or disemboweled in church, so that one part can be buried here, and another part, there.

42. A church ought to be reconciled when an infidel or a man who was publicly excommunicated is buried there, and at that time the walls are scrubbed down. In the preceding cases, in which a church ought to be reconciled, factual evidence should exist, or at least some report, that would lead to public reconciliation.[59]

43. The scandal, horror and abomination of indecent, sinful, and violent acts having been committed in a sacred place or in a church where one asks pardon for sins, where one seeking refuge should have protection, where the saving Host is immolated for sins, Leviticus, chapter 14 [cf. Lev 14:13], where those who are fleeing are saved, and where praises are offered to God—occasion the reconciliation, as does the intention and the will to commit mortal sin there.[60] If these things are done in secret, it is not necessary to reconcile it, because the church, since it is holy, cannot be defiled, or rather, the infamy of the deed cannot destroy the sanctity of the place; still, others think the opposite about this, that it should at least be reconciled in secret so that the wrongdoers are not publicly revealed.

44. And the reconciliation is done as an example and to cause fear, so that those seeing a church, which in no way has sinned, being washed and purified for the sin of another, will think to themselves how much more should they labor in the expiation of their own sins.

45. A cemetery in which a pagan or an infidel or an excommunicate is buried must be reconciled, and the bones buried there, if they can be distinguished from those of the faithful, should first be thrown out.[61] In the previous cases in which the church is reconciled, the cemetery is also reconciled for the same cases, for the cemetery has the same privileges which the church enjoys, as discussed under the heading *On holy unctions*;[62] for since it was blessed, it is a sacred place, and it is reconciled by a bishop in the same way as a church, through the solemn aspersion of blessed water mixed with wine and ashes.[63]

46. It should also be noted that in whatever part of the church or cemetery the violence or the pollution was perpetrated, all of the other parts of the church, on account of their connection with one another, are understood to be violated.[64] For though the consecration of the church, the altar, and the cemetery might be distinct, all of them nonetheless have one and the same privilege, which is not reserved for one part of the church or one corner, which is especially true if the church and the cemetery are connected.[65] If, however, one stands apart from the other, one can well be violated without the other. If one of their parts has been violated or polluted, then the other part is violated or polluted, and for the same reason, if one part is reconciled, the other parts are understood to be reconciled; since nothing is as natural as dissolving something in the same manner in which it was bound,[66] and the right of binding and loosing are the same;[67] and so, when the cemetery is violated or polluted, it suffices to reconcile the church. Nonetheless, some simply assert that the violation of one never causes the violation of the other, and as a consequence, whichever of them involved ought to be specifically reconciled; but they are opposed by the authority of the Pontificals in which a special form for reconciling a cemetery cannot be found.[68] Finally, if a church or a cemetery or some other thing is consecrated or blessed by an excommunicated bishop, such cases do not require reconciliation, since the sacraments performed by such a bishop in the foundation of a church are indeed true,[69] as discussed in the prologue of the third part.[70] But when, as said previously, the funeral rites of an excommunicate profane a cemetery or a church, it is indeed much more clear that the sacraments and the benedictions that are performed and pass through the mouth of the excommunicate—and what pertains to their merits—appear to be contaminated and besmirched before God; therefore it is appropriate that those places be reconciled before such sacraments are used by the faithful, which a reading of the sacred canons plainly teaches,[71] and as the Lord says through the Prophet: *I will curse your benedictions* [Mal 2:2].

{ 7 }

ON THE DEDICATION OF THE ALTAR

1. Not only is the church consecrated, but also the altar, and this is done for three reasons.[1] First, for the offering of sacrifices to God there, Genesis, chapter 8: *Noah built an altar for the Lord, and taking every clean bird and cattle, offered them on the altar* [Gen 8:20]. This sacrament (of the altar) is the Body and Blood of Christ which we immolate, in memory of His Passion, according to what is written: *Do this is in remembrance of me* [Lk 22:19].

2. Second, to invoke the name of God, as Genesis, chapter 12, says: *Abraham built an altar to God, who appeared to him, and there he invoked the name of the Lord* [Gen 12:7–8]. This invocation, which is done on the altar, is properly called the Mass.

3. Third, for singing, Ecclesiasticus, chapter 47: *And he gave him strength against his enemies, and he made singers stand facing the altar, and their sound made sweet melodies* [Sir 47:10–11].

4. The manner and order in which an altar is consecrated is as follows.[2] First, the bishop begins: "O God, come to my assistance,"[3] and afterwards, he blesses the water and then he makes four crosses with holy water on the four corners of the altar. Then he goes around the altar seven times, and seven times, he blesses the table of the altar with the sprinkling of blessed water with hyssop. The church itself is sprinkled and the remaining water is poured at the base of the altar; then, four crosses are made with chrism in the four corners of the sepulcher where the relics are to be placed, and then the relics are placed in a case with three grains of frankincense, and thus are they placed in the sepulcher.[4] Then a panel is placed over it, confirmed with the sign of the holy cross; and afterwards, the stone which we call the table is fitted to the top of

the altar, and having been placed there, it is anointed with oil in five places, and then it is anointed again, in the same manner as the oil, with chrism. The altar is confirmed with chrism in the front, where the sign of the cross is made, and incense is offered in five places. When this is done, the altar is covered and vested in clean linens and then the sacrifice is celebrated on it. Now let us follow up on each of these items one by one.

5. First, it must be noted that the altar is consecrated with an unction of chrism, with a blessing during the process; and that altar must be made entirely of stone. And thus the pontiff stands and says: "O God, Come to my assistance," since the Lord Himself says: *Without me you can do nothing* [Jn 15:5].

6. And since this dedication signifies those who are to be baptized, who after having received the faith, prepare themselves for combat, and who are still in the midst of sighs and struggles, "Alleluia" is not recited; those who are not baptized are not worthy of the praises of the angels, thus in the next-to-last chapter of Tobit: *And in its streets, alleluia shall be sung* [Tob 13:22].[5] After the consecration of the church and the altar is completed, "Alleluia" is sung, for when the specter of demons has been expelled, God should be praised there. Now when Christ ascended the altar of the cross, He destroyed death, while showing the glory of the Trinity, but He immediately sang "Alleluia" after His resurrection.

7. Second, concerning the blessing of the water, it should be noted that this sort of exorcism is done to put the enemy to flight. For this sort of blessing, four things are necessary, namely: water, wine, salt, and ashes. And this is on account of three reasons.

8. First, because there are four things that expel the enemy. The first is the effusion of tears, signified by the water; the second is spiritual joy, signified by the wine; the third is mature discernment, signified by the salt; the fourth is deep humility, signified by the ashes. The water is also penance; the wine, the joy of the spirit; the salt, wisdom, as was proven in the previous chapter; the ashes, the humility of penitence. And so it is said of the Ninevites, that their king himself *rose from his throne, was clothed in sackcloth and sat in ashes* [Jon 3:6]. And then David says: *Since I ate ashes as bread*, etc. [Ps 101:10]. And then Abraham: *Shall I speak*, he says, *to my Lord, since I am dust and ashes?* [Gen 18:27].

9. Second, the water is the people or all of humanity, since the many waters signify the many peoples; the wine, divinity; the salt, the doctrine of divine teaching, which is the salt of the Covenant; the ashes that are employed, the memory of the Lord's Passion; the wine mixed with water,

is Christ, who is God and man. Through faith in the Lord's Passion, which is provided through the teaching of divine law, the people are signified, and they are also signified in the water; they are joined in the union of faith to their head, God, and to man.

10. Third, it can be said that this blessed water signifies the Holy Spirit, without whose blowing, nothing can ever be sanctified, and without whose grace, there can be no remission of sins. The Truth Himself showed that the Holy Spirit should be called water, saying: *He who believes in me, rivers of living water will flow from within him* [Jn 7:38], which the Evangelist explains, saying: *He said this about the Holy Spirit, which those believing in Him would receive* [Jn 7:39].

11. And note the order of the sacrament: the church is consecrated outwardly with water, inwardly with the Spirit. This is what the Lord meant when He said: *Unless you are born again with water and the Holy Spirit*, etc. [Jn 3:5]. Behold the water, behold the Spirit: in the sacrament of Baptism, neither can there be water without the Spirit nor can there be the Spirit without water, which itself signified the Spirit, which in the first part of the creation of the world moved over the waters [cf. Gen 1:2]. With this water, the altar itself and the interior of the entire temple are sprinkled when the altar and the church are dedicated together.

12. Although the Spirit and water are sufficient for the completion of Baptism and the consecration of a church, nevertheless, the holy Fathers who established this practice wished to satisfy us not only with those things that pertain to the power of the sacrament but also with things that pertain to what it signifies; therefore, they added salt, wine, ashes, oil, and chrism. Indeed, Phillip did not have oil or chrism when he baptized the eunuch, Acts, chapter 8 [cf. Acts 8:38]. But neither of these should be lacking (oil and chrism), and they must be mixed together because the people of God, which is the Church, will neither be sanctified nor delivered from sin without these being joined together at the same time. This is touched upon under the heading *On consecrations*.[6] The need for water is certainly clear, because: *Unless someone is born again with water*, etc. [Jn 3:5].

13. Salt is needed whenever the water of Baptism is sprinkled, because without the seasoning of the faith, which is signified in this salt, no one can be saved. The wine designates the spiritual understanding of the divine law, which is why the Lord turned water into wine at the wedding [at Cana]. If anyone is not sprinkled with it, that is, if anyone does not drink of it or does not believe in the one offering the drink, he shall not enter into the blessedness of eternal life. And the aspersion of ashes,

through which is understood the humility of penance, is of such necessity that without it, the remission of sins cannot take place in adults; through the ashes one comes to Baptism, and the ashes are the only refuge for sinners after Baptism. Thus, with good reason it is called "Baptism," when the Lord said in the Gospel, that John came into the whole region of Galilee, *preaching the Baptism of penance for the remission of sins* [Mk 1:4]. And note that there are four types of holy water, which will be discussed in the fourth part, under the heading *On the aspersion of holy water.*[7]

14. When all of these ingredients are thoroughly mixed, the pontiff makes four crosses with this water in the four corners of the altar, and then one in the middle. The four crosses represent the fourfold charity that those who approach the altar should have, that is: the love of God, themselves, their neighbors, and their enemies. Concerning these four corners of charity, it says in Genesis, chapter 28: *You shall extend to the east and west, the northern and the southern regions* [Gen 28:14], and therefore, four crosses are made on the four corners of the altar to designate that Christ saved the four corners of the world through the cross. Second, they are made to signify the four ways by which we ought to carry the cross of the Lord: in our heart, through meditation; in our mouth, through confession; in our body, through its mortification; and on our face, through its frequent imprint.[8] The cross in the middle of the altar signifies the suffering that Christ underwent in the middle of the world, through which He achieved our salvation in the middle of the world, that is, Jerusalem.

15. Then the pontiff goes around the altar seven times. First, to signify that he himself must devote himself to the pastoral care of all people, and that he has to be vigilant, which is designated by his course around the altar. For that reason the text is sung: *The watchmen came upon me, who went around the city* [Song 3:3]; and he must ceaselessly watch over the flock entrusted to him. For as Gilbert[9] says, it is a ridiculous thing to be a blind watchman; a limping advance guardsman; a neglectful prelate; a foolish teacher; and a dumb preacher.

16. Second, the seven courses around the altar signify the seven steps associated with the sevenfold virtue of the humility of Christ that we ought to have, and by which we should frequently go. The first virtue is that from His riches, He was made poor; the second, that He was placed in a crib; the third, that He was put under the authority of parents; the fourth, that He bowed His head under the hand of a servant; the fifth, that He endured a thieving and treacherous disciple; the sixth, that He

meekly stood before an iniquitous judge; the seventh, that He prayed mercifully for those crucifying Him.

17. Third, the seven courses signify the seven journeys of Christ. The first was from heaven to the womb of His mother; the second, from the womb to the crib; the third, from the crib into the world; the fourth, from the world to the cross; the fifth, from the cross to the sepulcher; the sixth, from the sepulcher to underworld; the seventh, from under-world to heaven. And then the bishop sprinkles the altar.

18. The Apostle states what the altar in the Temple signifies: *For the temple of God is holy, and you are that temple* [1 Cor 3:16]. And if we are the temple of God we have an altar, and our altar is our heart; for the heart is to man what the altar is to the temple. On this altar there should be a sacrifice or praise and jubilation, according to the Psalmist: *My sacrifice to God is a contrite spirit,* etc. [Ps 50:19]; and on this altar there is a commemoration of the Body and Blood of the Lord; and from this altar, prayers ascend to heaven since God looks into our hearts. This altar is also sprinkled with water when the hearts of men are cleansed from sin through the preaching of the Gospel; and preaching is called water, according to the text: *Let all who are thirsty come to the waters* [Isa 55:1]. With this water, that is, the preaching of the Gospel and the sanctification of the Holy Spirit, the altar of the heart and the entire man are cleansed and sanctified. And then the altar of the heart is consecrated through the idea of fear, that it might be initiated into doing good, and also by the devotion of love, so that it might be confirmed in being better, for: *The beginning of wisdom is fear of the Lord* [Ps 110:10].

19. The altar is sprinkled with water seven times to denote that in Baptism, the seven gifts of the Holy Spirit are granted. It is also symbolizes that we must always bear the memory of Christ's Passion, for the seven sprinklings of water are the seven effusions of Christ's blood. The first was His circumcision; the second, was when He prayed, and His sweat became as drops of blood; the third, in the flogging of His body; the fourth, in the crowning of His head with thorns; the fifth, in the piercing of His hands; the sixth, in the nailing of His feet to the cross; the seventh, in the opening of His side. Some sprinkle it three times since one is baptized in the name of the Holy Trinity, or because the Church is purified from the sins of thought, speech, and deed, for which reason is recited: "Have mercy on me, O God."[10]

20. The aspersions of the sort discussed above are done with hyssop, through which herb, which is lowly, the humility of Christ is suitably designated, since the effusions of His blood discussed previously were

done with the hyssop of Christ's humility and His inextinguishable charity, with which the Catholic Church is cleansed. And this herb naturally grows in rock, and the humility of nature believes in Christ, the rock, for according to the Apostle: *And the rock was Christ* [1 Cor 10:4]; and the herb is warm by nature, and the humility of Christ enflames frigid hearts for doing the works of charity; and its roots penetrate stone and its humility breaks the hardness of heart of those who abstain from charity; it is good for the chest and a remedy against tumors, and it heals the tumor of pride; and it is born, reborn, and spreads its roots in the ground. For this reason, the whole multitude of the faithful can be understood by it, especially those who are rooted and established in their faith in Christ, who cannot be uprooted or separated from the love of Christ. We should understand that it is better for bishops and priests to show such qualities, since they hold a greater dignity in the Church, and they should be much more firmly attached to their faith in Christ; for by them, the water is sprinkled, and through them and by them the faithful in Christ are baptized; and it has been given to them to perform the sacrament of Baptism.

21. While the altar is being sprinkled with water the bishop sings: "My house is a house of prayer," and then: "I shall speak your name to my friends."[11] And because no work can be completed without God, he thus prays so that those entering this place to ask God's blessings will be heard. And then, while both the church and the altar are being consecrated, the entire church itself is sprinkled with water, as was already discussed in the previous chapter. When this is done, the bishop approaches the altar with the Psalm being chanted, and the rest of the water is poured out at the base of the altar, just as in the Old Testament, the remaining blood was poured onto the pedestal of that altar, which is the same as the base; this signifies that what remains, and what surpasses human resources in such a sacrament is commended to God, who is the High Priest, who provides for the defects of other priests. The sepulcher or the cavity in which the relics ought to be sealed signifies the golden urn filled with manna that had been placed in the Ark of the Covenant, as already noted under the heading *On the altar.*[12]

22. This sort of sepulcher, which some call a "confession," which is our heart, is consecrated with four crosses made with chrism, because there are four virtues described in the Book of Wisdom, namely: prudence, fortitude, temperance, and justice; and our heart is anointed, so to speak, with these virtues when we are prepared to receive the mysteries of the heavenly secrets through the gifts of the Holy Spirit. Happy is the soul

that is endowed with these virtues, for whom prudence provides counsel in difficult matters; fortitude gives assistance in adversity; temperance gives refuge against illicit things; and justice provides direction in
daily actions. And this sepulcher is sometimes on the top part of the
altar and sometimes on the front side.

23. Fittingly, there cannot be a consecration of a fixed altar without
the relics of Saints, or if none can be found there, without the Body of
Christ, but if it is a portable altar it can be consecrated without them.[13]
The relics are examples of both Testaments; authorities for the sufferings of the Martyrs and the lives of Confessors, that were left to us for
their imitation. We seal these in a case [capsa], so that we might retain
them in our heart to imitate them, which, if we hear and understand
their example and we do not do their works, this will work much more
towards our damnation than our salvation, since the hearers of the Law
are not righteous before God, but those who follow it; thus the Apostle
says: *Be my imitators just as I am an imitator of Christ* [1 Cor 11:1].

24. The solemn transport of relics is done in imitation of what we
read in Exodus [cf. Ex 25:13], that in the Ark of the Testament, there
were two gold rings that penetrated into the wood, and poles made of
shittim wood, overlaid with gold, that were placed through these rings
when the Ark was carried. And before the pontiff enters the church, he
goes around the church with the relics so that they can be the protectors
of that church. We read also in 3 Kings chapter 8 [cf. 1 Chr 8:1–5], that
when the Temple was dedicated, all of the ancient men of Israel, with
the princes of the tribes, and heads of the families were gathered before
King Solomon in Jerusalem, so that they might carry the Ark of Covenant of the Lord; and all of the elders of Israel came. The priests then
brought the Ark of the Covenant of the Lord into its place, into the oracle of the Temple, the Holy of Holies, under the wings of the cherubim,
since the cherubim spread their wings over the place where the Ark was
and protected it and the poles attached to it. King Solomon and the
whole multitude of the people of Israel who had come to him walked
with him toward the Ark. And today, in memory of this event, the prelates, magnates, and people of the province come together for the dedication of churches, and follow in procession the bishop who is consecrating it, and the relics are solemnly carried under a little tent [papilio]
or an umbrella [umbraculum]. Then the pontiff, before entering the
church with those who accompany him, gives a sermon to the people;
for when the Ark had been carried to its place, Solomon turned his face
toward the people and blessed the whole gathering of Israel, and he

prayed for those who would pray in the Temple, and the whole assembly of Israel stood and Solomon said: *Blessed be the Lord God of Israel*, etc. [1 Chr 8:15], as we read there.

25. The relics of saints are sealed in a little case with three grains of frankincense because we must retain in our memory the examples of the saints, with their faith in the Trinity, that is, the Father, Son, and Holy Spirit. For we must believe in one God, one faith, and one Baptism, because: *The just man lives by faith, without which* [Gal 3:11], as the Apostle says, *it is impossible to please God* [Heb 11:6]. Some sort of panel is placed on the top and is attached to this sepulcher, fortified with a sign of the cross made with chrism; for the chrism is understood to mean the gift of the Holy Spirit, with which the panel, that is, charity, is anointed, because our heart is fortified with the grace of the Holy Spirit so that we can observe the heavenly secrets. Then this panel, fortified with this sign, is placed on top of the relics, because through the example of the saints charity is inflamed, which covers a multitude of sins just as the panel covers the relics, and so the Apostle says: *The charity of God is poured forth in our hearts through the Holy Spirit who has been given to us* [Rom 5:5]. And this panel or stone contains or is called the "seal of the sepulcher," just as Pope Alexander III says.[14] And afterwards the stone, which is called the table of the altar, is attached to the altar, through which we can understand the perfection and solidity of the knowledge of God; this table ought to be made of stone, not on account of its hardness but because of the solidity of the faith, just as the Lord said to Peter: *You are rock, and upon this rock*, that is, on the strength of this faith, *I will build my Church* [Mt 16:18].

26. Just as the table is the completion and perfection of the altar, so too is the knowledge of God the completion and perfection of all good works. Thus it says in Wisdom, in reference to God: *For to know You is the completion of justice and to know Your justice and strength is the root of all immortality* [Wis 15:3]. And the Lord says through Jeremiah: *Let him who glories glory in this, to know and know of Me* [Jer 9:24].

27. And we understand the stone itself to be Christ, about whom the Apostle says: *Jesus Christ Himself is the chief corner stone* [Eph 2:20], and through the same stone the humanity of Christ is designated. In Daniel we read that a stone was cut from the mountain without human hands [cf. Dan 2:45], because Christ was miraculously born, without the seed of a man, of the Blessed Virgin, who on account of her lofty virtue is called a mountain; and Christ became a great mountain and filled the entire world. The Psalmist speaks of this: *The stone that the builders re-*

jected has been made the cornerstone [Ps 117:22], because Christ, whom the builders rejected, that is, the Jews, said: *We do not want him ruling over us* [Lk 19:27],[15] and He became the cornerstone, because as the Apostle said: *God exalted Him and gave Him a name which is above every other name* [Phil 2:9]. Or, the stone is understood to mean charity, as was previously said, which ought to be great and extensive, because the command to be charitable extends broadly, even to enemies, according to the precept of the Lord: *Love*, He says, *your enemies* [Lk 6:27].

28. Altars are never anointed unless they are made of stone, because Christ, whom the altar signifies, is the stone that grows into a mountain, as we just said. He Himself is the full mountain, anointed with the oil of gladness, above his fellow rulers [cf. Ps 44:9]. Nevertheless, we read in Exodus that the Lord commanded that altars be built of *shittim* wood, which is incorruptible; and the altar of the Lateran basilica is wooden. Solomon made a golden altar, as we read in 3 Kings, chapter 7 [cf. 1 Chr 7:48], but these altars were only made as figurative signs. And in the County of Provence, in the castle of Saint-Mary-on-the-Sea, there is an earthen altar there that was made by Mary Magdalene and Martha, and Mary the mother of James and Mary the mother of Salome.

Then, after the altar is sprinkled with baptismal water, what remains is for it to be smeared with oil and chrism. The bishop then pours oil and chrism on it and sings: "Jacob erected a stone monument, pouring oil on top of it."[16] That church was itself a prototype for the other churches: *Because from Zion shall go forth the Law, and from Jerusalem, the word of the Lord* [Isa 2:3].

29. First, [the bishop] makes five crosses on the altar with the oil of the sick, according to the Roman Ordinal;[17] but according to the custom of other churches, using either oil, he makes a cross in the middle and four crosses on the corners; and then afterwards, he does the same thing over again with the chrism. Fittingly, we understand the oil to be the grace of the Holy Spirit, about which the Prophet Isaiah says: *The yoke has dissolved from the oil of his face* [Isa 10:27]; just as the bishop pours oil onto the altar, so Christ, who is our High Priest, pours grace onto our altar, which is our heart, for He is the dispenser of all graces through the Holy Spirit, just as the Apostle says: *To one is given a word of wisdom, to another a word of knowledge, to another a word of faith, to another the grace of healing* [1 Cor 12:8–9]. And just as the bishop purifies the table of the altar with oil, so too does the Holy Spirit purify our heart from all of its vices and sins.

30. Christ was also anointed with oil; not, however, with one that was visible but one that was invisible, that is, with the grace of the Holy Spirit; thus David says: *He has anointed you with the oil of gladness above your fellow rulers* [Ps 44:8], that is, more than all of the saints who were partakers of His grace, that is, of Christ. It follows that this anointing pertains more specifically to Christ than the others since God anointed Him above all others to possess the fullness of good works; therefore, He is called "the anointed one." The anointing done with oil also signifies mercy, according to the Gospel: *Anoint your head and wash your face* [Mt 6:17]; just as oil does in liquids, so too does mercy rise above good works, and when you pour oil into whatever sort of liquid, it always floats to the top. Concerning mercy, it is written: *The Lord is sweet to all, and His mercies are above all his works* [Ps 144:9], *and mercy surpasses judgment* [Jas 2:13]. This oil also smears the altar of our heart, that always mindful of mercy, we will not lose the effects of the sprinkling of water and the regeneration of Baptism.

31. The five crosses of oil signify that we should also bear the memory of the five sufferings of Christ that He bore for us. For He Himself bore five wounds on our account, namely: on His hands, feet, and side; and they designate the five types of mercy that are necessary to us.

32. For it is necessary that man pity Christ, suffering His Passion with Him, as Job says, in the place of Christ: *Pity me, pity me,* etc. [Job 19:21]. It is necessary that he have pity for his neighbor when he endures evil, as in Ecclesiasticus: *Compassion of man for his neighbor* [Sir 18:12]. And for himself, he should have pity, for three reasons, namely: for the things committed, while lamenting them, as in Jeremiah: *There is no one who does penance for his sins by saying, What have I done?* [Jer 8:6]; for the things he has omitted, as Isaiah says: *Woe is me, I have been silent* [Isa 6:5], that is, because I have not spoken, as if he said: because I did not do the good that I was able to do. And pity for the good deeds done with less than pure intentions, as Luke says: *When we have done all of our good works, let us say that we are useless servants* [Lk 17:10], as if he said: we have done good works but have not done them well, not with pure intentions; and therefore, we have done them uselessly, just as he who gives alms, but for vainglory does good, but does not do it well or with purity. Ecclesiasticus speaks of this threefold pity: *Pity your soul to be pleasing to God* [Sir 30:24]. Since spiritual compassion must accompany the performance of a good work, two crosses are made: the first, with oil, the other, with chrism, thus the Psalmist says: *Blessed is he who shows pity and provides help* [Ps 111:5], who has pity in his soul and pro-

vides help with his good work. And since it does not suffice to have spiritual compassion with the performance of a good work without the odor of good repute, according to the Gospel: *Let your light shine so that God may be glorified* [Mt 5:16], therefore, the five crosses are made with chrism, which consists of balsam and oil.

33. Because of its good odor, balsam signifies a good reputation; the oil, on account of its clarity, the sharpness of conscience that we must have, for according to the Apostle: *Our glory is the testimony of our conscience*[18] [1 Cor 1:12]. Thus the balsam is fittingly mixed with the oil when the good odor of one's repute is added to mercy.

34. Moreover, through the five crosses of oil and chrism we understand the five senses of our body, which are doubled and grow to ten; for when using the five bodily senses well, we guard them in ourselves and in others, confirmed in good works through our example and our instruction, and thus the good trader boasted, saying: *Behold, I have added another five* [Mt 25:20]. While these unctions are being done, they sing: "The Lord, your God has anointed you,"[19] which is sung in reference to Christ. The altar is anointed three times; twice with oil, and a third time with chrism, because the Church is marked with faith, hope, and charity, which is greater than the others; and when the chrism is poured out, we sing: "Behold, the odor of my son is like the odor of a fertile field."[20] This field is the Church, which springs with flowers, which shines with virtues, which is fragrant with works; where there are the roses of Martyrs, the lilies of Virgins, the violets of Confessors, and the verdure of novices.[21] After the anointings, incense is burned, which signifies the devotion of prayer, or one who has the seven gifts of the Holy Spirit, who, being assimilated to God, can offer Him a devout prayer, whose image he is.

35. The incense is burned in five places, namely: in the four corners of the altar and in the middle, because we must employ the five bodily senses so that the renown of our good works will be extended to our neighbor. Regarding this, the Apostle says: *We are the good fragrance of Christ in all places* [2 Cor 2:15]; and in the Gospel: *Let your light shine before men that they may see your good works* [Mt 5:16]. And besides, this frequent use of incense is the continual dialogue between Christ the priest and pontiff and God the Father, done on our behalf.

36. A cross is made with incense to show His suffering before God and to call on Him on our behalf. The copious burning of incense in the corners and in the middle of the altar is the multiplication of prayers in Jerusalem and in the universal Church.

37. Then, the altar is confirmed with the sign of the cross while saying: "Confirm, O Lord,"[22] etc.; and this confirmation, made with chrism by the pontiff at the front of the stone, signifies the confirmation that is made daily by the Holy Spirit on the altar of our heart, so that no tribulation can separate our heart from the charity of God. Thus the Apostle says: *Who can separate us from the charity of Christ? Neither tribulation, nor distress*, etc. [Rom 8:35]. And "Glory to the Father" is added to sing the praise of the Trinity.

38. The final blessing of the altar signifies that final blessing in which is said: "Come to me, O blessed ones," etc.[23] Then, the altar is wiped with white linen to denote that our body must be cleansed with a chaste life. Then the vessels, vestments, and the linens assigned to the divine cult are blessed; for Moses was taught by the Lord, for forty days, how to make the linens and ornaments necessary for the Temple.

39. Indeed, to bless the utensils of the church is to render our works to God. Afterwards, the altar is vested with clean, white cloths, which is treated under the heading *On the altar*.[24] Then, the church is decorated and the lamps and candles are lit; at last, the works of the just shall shine brightly, and at last, the just shall gleam, and they shall dart about like sparks in a thicket [cf. Wis 3:7]. And then, a Mass is celebrated on the altar that has been consecrated in this manner, and the sacrifice is offered to the Most High; that sacrifice about which the Prophet spoke when he said: *My sacrifice to God is a contrite spirit* [Ps 50:19], which is discussed in the prologue of the fourth part.[25] There should not be a consecration without a Mass, according to Pope Gelasius,[26] for therein is revealed the sacrament that was hidden from the angels since the beginning. And note that during the sprinkling of the basilica, the pontiff only uses linen and ordinary vestments, but for the Mass, he is dressed in pontifical vestments that are the most costly, thereby recalling that the Priest of the Old Law used to purify the sanctuary dressed in linens, and after washing it, was dressed in pontifical vestments and offered the holocaust of the ram. But, because he was dressed in linens when he would send the scapegoat out after the purification, some clergy use simple vestments and wear linens when they consecrate a baptismal font or in the immersion of catechumens, where their sins are transformed.

{ 8 }

ON CONSECRATIONS AND UNCTIONS

1. We read [cf. Ex 30:22–29] that the Lord commanded Moses to make a chrism with which he would anoint the Tabernacle as well as the Ark of the Covenant, the table, and the vessels, on the day of dedication, and with which he could also anoint the priests and kings.[1]

2. We do not read, however, that Moses himself was anointed, as was Christ, unless we mean a spiritual anointing. Still, Christ wished for us to be anointed with a material unction so that we could attain the spiritual unction that is attached to the material; therefore, our merciful Mother Church provides us with diverse anointings. And here we shall touch on these by discussing: first, what unctions of this sort signify; second, by whom they are done; third, the anointing of those who are to baptized; fourth, the anointing of those who have just been baptized, which is done on the forehead by a bishop; fifth, the anointing of one who is about to be ordained; sixth, the anointing of a bishop about to be consecrated, or that of a prince; seventh, the anointing of a church, altar, chalice, or other objects for ecclesiastical ministry; eighth, extreme unction; ninth, on the consecration and blessing of a cemetery, vestments, and other ecclesiastical ornaments; tenth, on the consecration and blessing of virgins.

3. Concerning the first point,[2] it should be noted that there are two types of unction: the exterior, which is material or corporeal and is visible, and the interior, which is spiritual and invisible; the body is visibly anointed exteriorly, while the heart is invisibly anointed interiorly. Regarding the first one, the Apostle James says: *Is there one among you who is sick? Let him bring in the presbyters of the Church, and let them pray over him, anointing him with oil in the name of the Lord, and the prayer*

of faith shall save the sick man [Jas 5:14–15]. Regarding the second one, the Apostle John says: *And let the anointing, which you have received from him remain in you. And you have no need for someone else to teach you; but just as his unction teaches you concerning all things*, etc. [1 Jn 2:27]. The external unction is a sign of the interior one; the interior one is not only a sign, that is, a symbol of something, but is indeed a sacrament because if it is worthily received, it does or provides what it designates, that is, salvation, according to what is written: *They shall place their hands on the sick and they shall be made well* [Mk 16:18].

To which end it should be noted that two oils are blessed to show this exterior and visible unction, namely: the holy oil, or the oil of catechumens with which they are anointed, and the oil of the sick with which the sick are anointed. This unction is defined on the authority of the text: *Is there one among you who is sick?* etc. [Jas 5:14]. How the blessing of the oils and the chrism is done will be discussed in the sixth part, under the heading *On the fifth day of Holy Week*.[3]

4. But we should ask: why do we anoint the sick and the catechumens with oil? I respond: it is because invisible things are more easily grasped through visible things, just as the oil, while putting sickness to flight, rejuvenates the limbs of the weary, and on account of its own nature, sheds its light; it must then be believed that an unction with consecrated oil, which is a sign of faith, while putting sin to flight, provides health to the soul and shows its own light to it. Indeed, the visible oil, in the sign, is the invisible oil in the sacrament and the spiritual oil within the man. What concerns the oil of the sick we receive on the authority of the Apostles; what concerns the oil of catechumens, we receive on the authority of their apostolic successors.

5. And though it is possible that God can bestow spiritual oil without a corporeal quality, the Apostles nonetheless anointed the sick in this [corporeal] manner, as their successors anointed the catechumens; thus the practice that they consecrated by their own authority cannot be omitted without sinning, as noted already under the heading *On the altar*.[4] In the same way, in ancient times, the just were able to please God without circumcision, but afterwards, it was decreed to them that they be circumcised, and those neglecting to do this would fall into sin.

Third, we must speak of the unction of those who are to be baptized. And indeed, in the New Testament, not only were kings and priests anointed, as will be discussed, but everyone was, because with His Blood, Christ made us kings and priests before our God, that is, royal priests, according to what the Apostle Peter said: *You are a chosen peo-*

ple, that is chosen from among all nations of men, *a royal priesthood*, that is, when you rule yourselves well [1 Pet 2:9].[5]

6. All Christians are anointed twice before Baptism, but the blessed oil is first put on the breast, and then between the shoulders; and then twice after Baptism, but with holy chrism—first at the top of the head, and then on the forehead by the bishop; and according to Augustine, the first three anointings were introduced more through custom than some Scriptural text.[6] The one being baptized is first anointed in the breast, which is the locus of the heart, so that through the gift of the Holy Spirit he will give up his error and ignorance and will take up the true faith, because: *The just man lives by faith* [Rom 1:17] and *with the heart, one believes in justice* [Rom 10:10]. And he is anointed between the shoulders so that through the grace of the Holy Spirit, he casts off his negligence and his sluggishness and practices doing good works, since: *Faith without works is dead* [Jas 2:26], and through the sacrament of faith, the thoughts in his breast will be cleansed, and through the practice of his works, he will have the strength for his labors; between the shoulders, since according to the Apostle, faith operates with love [cf. Gal 5:6].

And again, the oil is placed on the breast so that the faith will always remain in the heart, and so that the heart's faith and piety are never forgotten; and because it does not suffice simply to have faith in mind without expressing it in works, the anointing is between the shoulders, which signifies works. The oil also passes from the heart to the shoulders when the faith, which the mind conceives, is perfected in works.

And the one baptized is anointed with chrism at the top of the head by the priest, so that he will be prepared to provide a rationale for his faith to all who ask him, for the head is understood to be the mind, according to what we read: *The eyes*—that is, the intellect—*of the wise man are in his head*—that is, in his mind [Eccl 2:14]; this means that the higher part of the mind is reason and the lower part is feeling; thus reason is well understood as the crown, which is the top of the head, as reason is the higher part of the mind. More is said about this in the sixth part, under the heading *Holy Saturday*, where Confirmation is treated.[7] Therefore, before Baptism, the anointing is done with holy oil and after Baptism, with holy chrism, since chrism is only suitable for a Christian.

7. The word "Christ" comes from "chrism," or rather, it is from Christ that the term chrism is derived, not according to the form of the word but according to the rule of faith. For Christians derive their name from Christ, just as those anointed are derived from the "Anointed one," namely Christ, as all who run to the odor of His ointment, that is, of

Christ, whose name is oil that is poured forth; but according to the true meaning of the name, the word "Christian" comes from "chrism," according to Isidore.[8] More is said about this in the prologue of the second part.[9]

8. According to St. Augustine,[10] the unction with oil shows us that we are fully prepared to hear the faith, and that we are called to the good odor of Christ, and that we are reminded to renounce the Devil. The second unction, on the breast and between the shoulders is done, according to Rhabanus,[11] so that we will be fortified through the faith in all our members to perform good works, strengthened through the grace of God. Certainly, the breast means the power of faith; the shoulders, on which burdens are carried, the strength and the works of man, according to what is written: *They bind together unbearable burdens and place them on the shoulders of men*, etc. [Mt 23:4].

And the unction is done on the breast and between the shoulders so that in mind and in deed, the works of the Devil are disregarded, or on the breast so that it can be capable and strong enough to understand the word of God; and between the shoulders, so that he be strong enough to carry his yoke and the burden of the Law. And according to Rhabanus, either of these unctions is done in the form of a cross, so that at that point, the Devil recognizes the sign of his destruction, that is, the holy cross by which he is destroyed, on what was his original vessel; and now in succession, he knows himself to be estranged from that place, that is, that the anointed man is alienated from him.

9. This unction is done on the crown, that is, at the top of the head, on the cerebrum, according to the same author,[12] so that the one anointed may be joined to those who share in the kingdom of heaven, and because the soul of the one who is baptized is betrothed to its head, that is, Christ; moreover, it is done with chrism made from oil and balsam so that we might know that the Holy Spirit, which works invisibly, is given to him. For oil warms weary members and provides light, as was noted above, and balsam gives off a sweet scent. Seeing that the soul's members are weary when one does penance for having turned against God, the Holy Spirit comes to it, and illumines its understanding, and shows it the sins that have been remitted or must be remitted; and the Spirit gives him good works which provide a good odor for others, which is designated by the fragrant balsam. This anointing is also done on the crown of the head, where the seat of pride [*superbia*] is seen, which always seeks after higher things [*superiora*], so therefore, it is done in the form of the cross and in the name of humility.

10. Pope Sylvester[13] instituted that this unction can be done by priests when someone is at the point of death; thus it is credible that before his time, either type of unction, namely on the crown and on the forehead, was reserved for a bishop. When the bosom of the Church was extended, and the bishops could not meet everyone for Confirmation, this pope decreed, lest anyone die without the unction of chrism, they could be anointed by priests on the crown, on the cerebrum, which is the seat of wisdom, for their strength and the increase of grace. Thus, if they died afterwards, as Sicardus said in the *Mitrale*,[14] they receive the proportion of glory established by the increase of their grace.

11. Nevertheless, we believe that without receiving the unction, one can be saved by Baptism alone; and the Holy Spirit can be given to anyone to whom God wishes to give it, as we read in the Acts of the Apostles.

12. Still, the Arnaldists,[15] those faithless heretics, assert that men never receive the Holy Spirit through the Baptism of water, nor did the Samaritans receive the Holy Spirit when they accepted the imposition of hands.

13. It can also be said, according to Rhabanus,[16] that all unctions done in the breast are done with the invocation of the Holy Trinity, so that no traces of the enemy will remain hidden in the breast, but rather, with faith in the Holy Trinity, the mind will be strengthened, and it will receive and have an understanding of the commandments of God. Any of the faithful are anointed twice: first, once with oil; afterwards, two times with chrism.[17] The first comes with Baptism, on top of the head; the second one, after Baptism, on the forehead, namely in Confirmation, because the Holy Spirit was given to the Apostles twice, as will be discussed in the sixth part, under the heading *On Holy Saturday*.[18]

In the fourth place, the anointing that the bishop does on the forehead of the one baptized ought to be discussed, but this will be done in the sixth part, under the heading *On Holy Saturday*.[19]

14. In the fifth place, concerning the unction of someone being ordained, it should be noted that the hands of the priest are anointed by the bishop, so that he understands that in this sacrament, he receives the power and the grace to consecrate; thus, while anointing his hands, the bishop says: "Deign, O Lord, to consecrate and sanctify these hands through this unction and our blessing, so that whatever they consecrate shall be consecrated, and whatever they bless shall be blessed in the name of the Lord."[20] Therefore, devout men kiss the hands of priests immediately after their ordination, believing, through this act, that they will

participate in their prayers and good works. And the hands are anointed with oil, so that they can do the works of mercy that they ought to do for all men through their strength; for the hands designate works while the oil designates mercy. Thus, the Samaritan, coming upon the wounded man, poured wine and oil into his wounds [cf. Lk 10:34]. The hands are also anointed with oil so that they might be moistened when offering the sacrifice to God for our sins, and to maintain them lavishly—not aridly and lowly—for the performance of the other duties of piety.[21] And the oil designates either the grace of healing or the love of charity. Therefore, an imposition of hands is done with the oil on the head of the ordinand, because by the hands we understand good works; through the fingers, the gifts of the Holy Spirit; through the head, the mind. There is also the imposition of hands because he whose mind is imbued with the gifts of the Holy Spirit is sent forth to do the works of Christ.

15. Sixth, concerning the unction of bishops and princes, it should be known that the anointing of a bishop has its origins in the Old Testament, for in Leviticus, chapter 21, it says: *The pontiff, upon whose head the oil of unction has been poured, and whose hands have been consecrated to the priesthood* [Lev 21:10]. The bishop is fittingly anointed with the chrism, which, as previously noted, is made with oil and balsam; and he is anointed in body and in heart: so that in his interior he has a shining conscience before God, designated by the oil; and on the exterior, he has the odor of a good reputation with his neighbor, which is designated by the balsam. Concerning[22] this shining conscience, the Apostle says: *Our glory is this, the testimony of our conscience* [2 Cor 1:12]; for all glorious is the king's daughter as she proceeds within [cf. Ps 44:14]. Concerning the odor of a good reputation, the same Apostle says: *We are the odor of Christ*, that is, the example and imitation of Christ, *in all places*, and *we are for others an odor of life that leads to life* [2 Cor 2:15–16], as if he says: we are the example of love and of good works leading to eternal life, while others are an odor of death that leads to death [cf. 2 Cor 2:16], that is, the odor of envy and evil thoughts that lead to eternal death.

16. The bishop[23] must be of good repute among those who are inside and outside the doors of the Church; just as a curtain, that is, the faithful, draws another curtain, that is the faithless, to the faith. And the one who hears, coming to learn and believe, can say, "I have come," namely, "to preach and teach." The head and hands of the bishop are consecrated with this ointment; for through the head the mind is represented, according to the text of the Gospel: *Anoint*, that is, humble, *your head and face*, that is, your conscience, and *wash* [your face], namely, with tears

[Mt 16:17]. Works are designated by the hands, according to the Canticle of Canticles: *My hands*, that is, good works, *were dripping with myrrh* [Song 5:5], that is, they gave a good example to others.

17. The head is also anointed with the balsam of charity; first, so that the bishop will love God with his entire heart, his entire mind, and his entire soul; and also, with the example of Christ, loving his neighbor as he loves himself. According to Gregory: "Oil on the head is charity in the mind."[24] Second, the head is anointed to denote authority and dignity, because the unction not only creates a bishop but also a king. Third, to show that he is His vicar, that is, of Christ, and to represent Him, about which is spoken by the Prophet: *It is like an ointment on his head*, etc. [Ps 132:2]. The head of man is Christ; the head of Christ is God, who says of Himself: *The Spirit of the Lord is upon me, he who has anointed me; he has sent me to bring good news to the poor* [Lk 4:18]. Christ, our head, was anointed with invisible oil; He speaks for the universal Church, while the bishop speaks on behalf of those things entrusted to him.

18. His hands are anointed on account of his ministry and office. Indeed, the hands, which signify works, are anointed with oil, that is, with the chrism of piety and mercy, so that the bishop can do good for all people, but especially for those who are servants of the faith [cf. Gal 6:10]; so that his hands will be closed to none and opened to all, according to what is written: *She opens her hand to the destitute, and she extends her arm to the poor* [Prov 31:20]. The dry hand, the avaricious hand, the hand crippled by stinginess: this hand cannot be opened. The hands are also anointed so that they might be healed, that they might be opened, and that they might lavish alms on the needy. Second, so that it can be shown that they receive the power for blessing and consecrating; thus, the one consecrating his hands says: "Deign, O Lord, to consecrate and sanctify these hands" etc., as said above.[25] Third, that they might be cleansed for offering the sacrifices for our sins. And note that the hands of the bishop were anointed with oil when he was ordained a priest, and they are once more anointed with chrism when he is consecrated bishop. Good works are designated by the hands; the Holy Spirit or an abundance of grace, by the oil; by the balsam, which is mixed with oil in the chrism, the odor of good repute. Thus, Ecclesiasticus, chapter 24: *My odor is like a pure balsam* [Sir 24:21]. The gifts of the Holy Spirit ought to be manifested and the odor of good repute sensed in the works of bishops and others of superior rank more than in those of inferior rank, according to 2 Corinthians, chapter 2: *We are the odor of Christ for God* [2 Cor 2:15]; for in the celestial hierarchy, the higher order of angels is

more conspicuous with its exalted gifts and grace.[26] Therefore, in the consecration of their hands, though they have elsewhere been anointed with oil, it is reasonable for them to be anointed with chrism.

19. The thumb is also confirmed with chrism, so that the imposition of this thumb will serve for the salvation of all.

20. Clearly, in the Old Testament, not only was the priest anointed but also the king and prophet, just as we find in the Book of Kings, when the Lord decreed to Elias: *Go and return to your home, through the desert, to Damascus, and when you come there, anoint Hazael to be king over Syria, and you shall anoint Jehu, son of Namsi, to be the king over Israel. And Eliseus, the son of Saphat, who is from Abel, you shall anoint to be your prophet* [1 Chr 19:15–16]. Samuel also anointed David for the kingship. But after Jesus the Nazarene—whom God anointed with the Holy Spirit, as we read in the Acts of the Apostles [cf. Acts 10:38]—was anointed with oil above his companions, who, according to the Apostle, is the head of the Church that is His body [cf. Eph 5:23], the anointing of princes was transferred from the head to the arm, so that the prince, since the time of Christ, is not anointed on the head but on the arm or shoulder, or at the joint of the arm, in which princely dominion is fittingly designated, according to what is written: *And the dominion has been put on his shoulders* [Isa 9:6]. This is what was signified when Samuel had his shoulder placed before Saul, to whom he had given a place at the head of the table before all who had been invited [cf. 1 Kings 9:22]. Still, the sacramental smearing of oil on the head of the pontiff is observed because in his pontifical office, he stands in place of the head, that is, Christ, who is the head of the Church.

21. The unction of a pontiff differs from that of a prince because the head of the pontiff is consecrated with chrism while the arm of the prince is smeared with oil, so that it can be shown what difference there is between the authority of the pontiff and the power of the prince. And note that, just as we read in the Gospel, a certain father of the household called his servants and gave each of them ten gold pieces [cf. Lk 19:13]; for which reason the calling of the servants is the canonical election of the bishop, which is done according to the Lord's call when he called Aaron. A gold piece is given to him when he who imposes his hands on him and gives him the text of the Gospel, saying: "Go, and preach;"[27] and when he first enters his episcopal city, he bears the Gospel on his breast, according to the custom of some churches, showing how he will manage his gold pieces. But in some other churches, when the archbishop gives him his staff, he says: "Go, and preach," and the bishop immedi-

ately blesses the people, which signifies that Moses was sent to Egypt with a staff.

22. Bishops still follow the custom, on the day of their consecration, of riding white horses, covered with garments, representing what is read in Apocalypse, chapter 19: *And the armies that are in heaven followed him on white horses* [Rev 19:14]. Indeed, the armies that are in heaven are the good and just men and the prelates who daily, through celestial visions, follow after God in all of their good works; therefore, it can be said that they are in heaven because they only love and seek celestial things, hence the Apostle: *Our discourse is in heaven* [Phil 3:20]. These armies, that is, the good and just men and the prelates, follow Jesus when they conquer their vices through correction and by admonishing their neighbors. Thus James says: *He who causes a sinner to be converted from the error of his ways will free his soul from death*, etc. [Jas 5:20]. These armies are on white horses, that is, they are chaste in their bodies.

23. The bodies of the blessed are called horses, because just as horses are steered according to the will of the rider, so too are the bodies of the just ruled according to the will of Christ. These horses ought to be white or covered in white, that is, the bodies of the just and of the prelates ought to be chaste and pure; for if they are not chaste, they cannot follow Christ. And Peter says: *Christ has suffered for us, leaving us an example so that we may follow in his steps*, etc. [1 Pet 2:21]. And in fact, the clerics of the holy Roman Church, through a decree of the Emperor Constantine,[28] ride horses adorned with linens of the purest white color.

On what day a bishop ought to be consecrated, and why the Gospel book is placed on the shoulders of the one being consecrated is discussed in the second part, under the heading *On the bishop*.[29]

In the seventh place,[30] we should discuss the unction of the church, altar, chalice and the other things associated with the ministries of a church, which, according to custom, are anointed when they are dedicated. And this is done not only according to the mandate of divine law, but also because Moses sprinkled the Tabernacle and all of the vessels for ministry with blood, and everything was thoroughly cleansed with blood; and so too is this done following the example of Blessed Sylvester,[31] who, when he consecrated an altar, used to anoint it with chrism. The Lord also decreed that Moses make oil with which he would anoint the Tabernacle of the Covenant, the table, the Ark of the Covenant, the candelabra, and the utensils, Exodus, chapters 30 and 40, and other things, as previously noted. These unctions are done so that those things that are anointed will be shown greater reverence, and a greater grace will be poured into them. These unctions have been discussed and will be discussed in their proper places.

24. A paten is consecrated and anointed for the ministry of the Body of Christ, who chose to be immolated on the altar of the cross for the salvation of all people; and our omnipotent God commanded that the bread of His image be borne to His altar on gold and silver patens. The chalice is also consecrated and anointed, so that the grace of the Holy Spirit will make it a new sepulcher for the Body and Blood of Christ, so that He will deign to fill it with His virtue; He who filled the chalice of Melchizedech, His servant.

25. In the eighth place, we must discuss Extreme Unction, which according to the decree of Pope Felix IV, and the precept of James the Apostle, is given to those suffering in their final hours.[32] But some say, when discussing unction, that it is not a sacrament, properly speaking, such as the use of chrism put on the forehead or another spot, because, as they assert, it can be done repeatedly when praying over a man; and such a practice does not apply to the sacraments.[33] This unction can fittingly be done by one priest, if others cannot be present to assist him; and this unction can only remit venial sins,[34] according to the text of James: *Is anyone among you sick,* as quoted above [Jas 5:14]. This anointing is also done on different parts of the body for the reasons that we can infer from the prayers that are said; and this is especially true of the anointing of those places where the five human senses reside, so that whatever wrongs the sick person did through them will be wiped out through the power of this unction. We read, in some Ordinals, that someone who is about to be anointed has to be at least eighteen years of age, and that the sick person can only be anointed once per year, though he is sick many times; and that no one ought to be anointed unless he first shows that he is in possession of his faculties and that he asks for this unction with words or signs.[35] And we should not anoint the shoulders, since they have already be anointed in Baptism and are henceforth deprived of this sort of ministry; and that someone who has been confirmed should not be anointed on the forehead but on the temples of the head; nor should the hands of a priest be anointed on the inside but rather on the outside, since they were already anointed during his ordination. And if someone has been anointed by a bishop, he should not, out of respect for the bishop, be anointed yet again by a priest.[36] And if someone who was sick was anointed and then gets better, the places where he was anointed are

washed, and the water that is collected is tossed into a fire; if, however, he dies, the body is not washed on account of the recent anointing. And if the sick person is at the point of death, he is quickly anointed lest he die without unction.[37] And some penitents, who are about to die, put on a hair shirt and humbly lie down in ashes, as will be discussed in the sixth part, under the heading *On Ash Wednesday.*[38]

26. In the ninth place, the cemetery—which enjoys the same privileges as the church—is consecrated and blessed;[39] just as the Lord blessed, through the hands of His servants, Abraham, Isaac, and Jacob, the land that He had prepared as a sepulcher for the sons of Hebron [cf. Gen 35:27–29; Gen 50:13; Josh 14:15]. And it is blessed so that henceforth, it will cease to be the dwelling place of impure spirits, so that the bodies of the faithful may rest in peace there until the day of judgment, unless the bodies of pagans and infidels have been buried there; they cannot have peace until they are ejected.[40]

27. It should also be noted[41] that the altar linens, priestly vestments, and ecclesiastical furnishings of this sort must be blessed. We read that Moses, following the commandment of the Lord, sanctified the Tabernacle with divine prayers, along with the table, altar, vases, and utensils used for the fulfillment of the divine cult [cf. Gen 26: 1–16]. If the Jews, who served the Law in the shadow of future rites, used to do this—Hebrews, chapters 8 and 10 [cf. Heb 8:5; 10:1]—how much more should we, to whom the truth has been revealed through Christ, do such things. And these things are made holy by a bishop, not a "choir bishop" [*corepiscopus*];[42] and so we read in Exodus, in the next-to-last chapter, that Moses blessed all of the vases for the ministry [cf. Ex 39:43]. And if a small piece or a thread is added to a vestment it should not, on that account, be blessed again, as is proven by the testimony of the law.[43] The sacred vestments are discussed in the prologue of the third part.[44] And note that the blessing and consecration of churches and ecclesiastical vestments and ornaments is not done because those things themselves can receive grace, because they are inanimate objects, but because grace is known through them, as it were, to men; so that those things that are blessed and consecrated and placed in service of the divine cult, and rendered fitting for it, inspire a much greater reverence. A greater grace is poured out in the unction and blessing of a person. And some clerics raise their hands during the blessing of ecclesiastical ornaments, which is discussed in the second part, under the heading *On the deacon.*[45] The tenth topic that must be discussed is the consecration of virgins, but this is done the prologue of the second part.[46]

{ 9 }

ON THE ECCLESIASTICAL SACRAMENTS

1. With regard to the ecclesiastical sacraments, it should be noted that according to Gregory: "A sacrament exists when a thing is done in some solemn celebration that is a sign of something else that we receive; something that must be received reverently, that is, worthily."[1] We understand a mystery to be what is done in a hidden or invisible manner by the Holy Spirit, in such a way that He intimates Himself through His work, and He blesses as He sanctifies.

2. A mystery exists in the sacraments, while a ministry is in the ecclesiastical ornaments. And, according to Augustine: "A sacrament is an invisible grace in a visible form."[2] Similarly a sacrifice is visible, and a sacrament is invisible. Likewise, a sign is a thing whose outward appearance impresses our senses, and makes us come to the knowledge of another thing that it represents.[3]

3. A sacrament is also called a sign of a sacred thing, or a sacred secret. More is said about this in the fourth part, under the heading *The seventh part of the Canon*, where it says "The Mystery of Faith,"[4] and under the heading *On the oblation*.[5]

4. Some are sacraments of necessity only; some, of dignity and necessity; some, of order and necessity; some, of dignity and choice; some are only sacraments of choice.[6] The only sacrament of necessity is Baptism—and in extreme cases it can be administered by anyone, provided that the form established by the Church is used—which contributes to one's salvation;[7] and it is called a sacrament of necessity since without it, no one can be saved, if out of contempt it is forsaken. This sacrament is discussed in the sixth part, under the heading *Holy Saturday*.[8] The sacrament of dignity and necessity is Confirmation; it is a sacrament of

dignity since it can only be conferred by a bishop, and it is a sacrament of necessity, since he who renounces it out of contempt, will not be saved.[9] This is also discussed under the previously mentioned heading of *Holy Saturday.*[10]

5. The sacraments of order and necessity are Penance, the Eucharist, and Extreme Unction; they are sacraments of order since they can only be administered by those properly ordained according to the canons of the Apostolic Church,[11] unless in the case of an emergency, in which case someone can confess himself to a layman. And these are sacraments of necessity, since he who renounces them out of contempt, cannot be saved. For a discussion of Penance, see the sixth part, under the heading *On Holy Thursday,*[12] and we also discussed this in our *Repertorium*, under the heading "On penance and the remission of sin."[13] The Eucharist is discussed in the fourth part, under the heading *On the Canon of the Mass.* Extreme Unction was treated in the previous chapter.

6. The sacrament of dignity and choice is ordination: dignity, because it can only be conferred by a bishop, or because no one should be admitted to it as worthy unless he is indeed worthy; and of choice, because without it, one can be saved. More is said about this in the prologue of the second part.[14]

7. Marriage is a sacrament of choice only,[15] and it is called one of choice since one can be saved without it;[16] nor is it profitable for a man striving for the kingdom of Heaven to marry. It should be noted that according to the Church canons,[17] the solemn celebration of a wedding must not be done during Septuagesima,[18] which is a time of sorrow, up to the octave of Easter; nor should it be done during the three weeks before the Feast of St. John [the Baptist]. But, according to the general custom of the universal Church, marriage can be publicly contracted in a church from the morning of Low Sunday,[19] that is, from the octave of Easter, up to the first Rogation Day.[20] And from the morning of first Rogation Day, this solemnity is prohibited, and this prohibition lasts up to the eighth day after Pentecost, inclusive; thus did Pope Clement speak in his decretal letter.[21] And from the first Sunday of Advent up to the Feast of the Epiphany, weddings must not be celebrated, nor would they have been performed up to the octave of Epiphany,[22] unless the Lord had honored a wedding with both His presence and a miracle.[23] Thus, during that season, the hymn is sung: "Today, the Church is joined to her celestial husband."[24] Still, some say that is preferable that this prohibition be extended until the octave of this feast, along with the Office for the

conversion of the water into wine at the wedding. In those times enumerated above, matrimony is not contracted since those times are allotted to prayer.

8. And therefore, during this time, a man ought to be absent from his wife's bed; since, generally, during the time that one abstains from getting married, one must also abstain from conjugal love, unless, on account of human frailty, a man demands the conjugal debt from his wife, or she demands it from him; for they are not bound to this prohibition,[25] since according to the Apostle, a man does not have power over his body, but the woman does, and the same is true of her [cf. 1 Cor 7:4].[26] However, even though the solemn celebration of marriage is prohibited during these previously noted times, a lawful verbal contract for a marriage is considered legal from that point on, regardless of the time during which it was arranged.

But it was decreed in the canons,[27] that weddings cannot be celebrated in the three weeks that precede the Feast of Saint John the Baptist; and this was done so that this period would be more freely devoted to prayer. For the Church had instituted two other forty-day periods [quadragesimas] outside of the major period [i.e., Lent]: one was before the Feast of the Lord's Nativity, which is commonly called the "time of Saint Martin,"[28] which used to last up to the Feast of the Nativity; the other, was the forty days before the Feast of Saint John the Baptist, during which time one was devoted to praying, giving alms, and fasting. But, on account of human frailty, the two periods were combined into one; and once more it was divided into the three weeks of Advent, and the three weeks before the Birth of John the Baptist, during which time we must fast and abstain from conjugal union.

9. Moreover, according to Blessed Isidore,[29] women should be veiled when they marry so that they will know that they are always subject to their husbands; and, because when Rebecca saw Isaac, she covered her head [cf. Gen 24:65]. Also, after the blessing, the married couple is bound together with one woolen band, lest they disrupt the union, that is, the fidelity of the conjugal union. This woolen band has white and purple colors mixed together—the white is purity of life, and the purple applies to the future generation of this blood—that with this sign, each will at times remind the other of their continence and the law of the continent, and afterwards not refuse to render each other the conjugal debt.

10. Likewise, the ring is first given by the groom to his spouse for this reason: as a sign of their mutual love, or that by a pledge, that is, a sign,

their hearts may be joined. For this reason the ring is placed on the fourth finger, since in it there is a certain vein (as they say) that carries blood right to the heart.

11. Also, a certain wise man named Protheus[30] was the first, as a sign of his love, to make an iron ring, and therein placed a diamond; and then he established that the woman be in service of her betrothed, since just as iron rules over other metals, thus does love conquer all, because nothing is more powerful than the passion of love. And just as diamond is unbreakable, so too is love unconquerable, and this love is even as strong as death [cf. Song 8:6]; therefore, it became the norm to wear the ring on the finger which has the vein that comes from the heart. Later on, it became the custom to replace the iron with gold rings, and in place of diamonds, they were decorated with precious stones, because just as gold surpasses all other metals, so does love surpass all other possessions; and just as gold is decorated with precious stones, conjugal love is adorned with all of the other virtues. And, according to Ambrose,[31] marriage [*nuptie*] comes from the word that means, "to cover the head," [*obnubendo*]. For those [women] who marry are in the habit of covering their heads and not speaking out of modesty, which is why Rebecca, when she saw Isaac, to whom she was betrothed, began to cover her head [cf. Gen 24:65]. And modesty must precede a marriage, since more modesty preserves the union itself, and the woman must appear to have been more greatly desired by the man than the man by the woman. And, according to Jerome: "Lawful marriages are without sin, but during the time that conjugal acts are performed, the presence of the Holy Spirit is lacking, even if it were a Prophet doing the act of procreation."[32]

12. It should also be noted[33] that a threefold spiritual mystery [*sacramentum*][34] is designated by the carnal consummation of a marriage. The first mystery is the union of the faithful soul to God through faith, love and charity; or the union of the will to God, that is charity, which consists of one spirit between God and the just soul; thus the Apostle says: *He who clings to God is one in spirit with Him* [1 Cor 6:17]. This mystery is signified by the union of kindred souls when the first step—the betrothal—toward carnal matrimony is taken. The second is the union of human nature with God, which was done in the womb of the Virgin, through the Incarnation of the Word of God; or in the sharing between Christ and the Holy Church of that nature composed of flesh, to which these words apply: *The Word was made flesh*, etc. [Jn 1:14]. This mystery is designated in the consummation of carnal marriage, through the

union of bodies; not that the union itself, in which the Holy Spirit is not present, designates this mystery, but rather, that it is signified through the act of consummation. The third mystery is the unity of the Church, gathered from all nations and subjected to one man, Christ. This mystery is signified by the man who had only one wife, who was a virgin, and who afterwards was made a cleric and ordained.[35]

13. This is why one who is a bigamist or goes through with a second marriage is at that moment cut off from the unity of the Church, because he has divided his body among many; and because the symbolism of this third mystery does not belong to him, he cannot advance [to a second marriage], for this progression could not signify this unity. Besides, through his second marriage he withdraws from the prior matrimonial union. For the Church, which has joined herself to Christ, has never separated herself from Him, nor has He from her. A bigamist, therefore, can never signify such a unity; and thus justly, he can never be promoted to orders on account of his failure in this sacrament.[36]

14. And it should be noted, just as it was decreed at the Council of Carthage,[37] that the betrothed, who are about to be blessed, are offered to the Church and priest by their parents or a bridesmaid or groomsman. Having received their blessing, on that night, out of respect for their blessing, they should preserve their virginity.

15. To continue, marriages ought to be blessed with prayers and offerings by a priest, according to the decree of Pope Evaristus.[38] Still, if a man or woman goes through with bigamy by contracting another marriage, it must not be blessed by a priest; since they have already been blessed before, their blessing must not be repeated.[39] And marriages should not be blessed unless they are contracted by a male and female virgin, for the reason offered in the prologue of the second part.[40] And indeed, a priest who celebrates a wedding for a second wife is suspended from his office and his benefice, and must be sent to the Apostolic See, so that it can be known that he has been subjected to an exhortation to continence. According to the custom of some places, if someone contracts a marriage with a second virgin, the blessing is repeated; and this is done only if the Lord Pope knows and tolerates this, otherwise it has no validity. Some also say that if men have contracted marriage with virgins, without a blessing, being bigamists through this other contract, they can still be blessed; but, if those who contracted a marriage were blessed, even if they did not know each other carnally, if they contract another marriage, they are not blessed. The blessing of virgins is discussed in the prologue of the second part.[41]

16. It should also be noted that one sacrament can be more highly honored in its own right in four ways: namely, by reason of its efficacy, such as Baptism; by reason of its sanctity, such as the Eucharist; by reason of what it signifies, such as Marriage (although some do not approve of this manner of argument); and by reason of what it confers, such as Confirmation and Ordination.[42]

17. But one can ask: why were the sacraments instituted, since without them, God was able to give eternal life and grace to the human race? I respond that there are three reasons. First, for the humbling of man, so that man may reverently subject himself to insensate and inferior things, by the precept of God, and through this obedience, have greater merit before God. Second, for the sake of instruction, so that the mind will be instructed in the invisible virtue of that which must be known inwardly, when it perceives it outwardly through the visible appearance of the thing. Third, for the exercise of the mind; since man should never be idle, a useful and salutary exercise is put before him in the sacraments, through which he may avoid vain and harmful tasks, according to what is said: Always be doing some sort of work, so that the Devil will find you busy.[43] Thus, the sacraments should never be neglected, as noted in the preceding chapter.

NOTES

INTRODUCTION

1. Durand's name appears in several variant forms in scholarly literature. The medieval Latin spelling is most often *Durantis* or *Duranti*, and less frequently, *Durandus*. I have opted for the modern French spelling of his name, Durand, following the precedent set by editor of his famous *Pontificale*, Michel Andrieu (see n. 8).

2. There is still no complete modern biography of Durand. Though antiquated, there are two well-known surveys of his life and career: Victor Leclerq, "Guillaume Duranti, Évêque de Mende, surnommé le Spéculateur," in *Histoire Littéraire de la France* (Paris: Académie royale des Inscriptions et Belles-Lettres, 1895), 20:411–80; Louis Faletti, "Guillaume Durand," *Dictionnaire de droit canonique* 5 (1953): 1014–75. See also my entry, "William Durandus," in *Medieval Italy: An Encyclopedia*, ed. Christopher Kleinhenz (New York: Routledge, 2003), 2:1168–69. The most up-to-date bibliography for Durand studies can be found in Pierre-Marie Gy, O.P., ed., *Guillaume Durand, Évêque de Mende (v. 1230–1296): Canoniste, liturgiste et homme politique* (Paris: Éditions du Centre National de la Recherche Scientifique, 1992).

3. Situated in Langudeoc, in the Département de l'Hérault, Puimisson is about 10 km from the city of Beziers (very close to the Mediterranean coast).

4. William Durand, *Speculum iudiciale, illustratum et repurgatum a Giovanni Andrea et Baldo degli Ubaldi*, 4 parts in 2 vols. (Basel: Froben, 1574; repr., Darmstadt: Aalen, 1975).

5. Durand later produced a lengthy commentary on the decrees of the Second Council of Lyons: *In sacrosanctum Lugdunense concilium sub Gregorio X Guilelmi Duranti cognomento Speculatoris commentariis* (Fano: Simone Maiolo, 1569).

6. See Pierre-Marie Gy, O.P., "L'Ordinaire de Mende, une oeuvre inédite de Guillaume Durand l'Ancien," *Cahiers de Fanjeaux* 17 (1982): 239–49.

7. J. Berthelé and M. Valmary, "Les instructions et constitutions de Guillaume Durand le Spéculateur, publiées d'après le manuscrit de Cessenon," *Académie des Sciences et Lettres de Montpellier. Mémoires de la Section des Lettres*, 2nd ser., 3 (1905): 1–148. The one complete manuscript of this work was rediscovered in the late nineteenth century in the town of Cessenon, not far from Durand's birthplace. It is now preserved in the city of Mende, where Durand served as bishop. I have examined it

personally, and it appears that some of the marginal notes were written by Durand himself.

8. Michel Andrieu, ed., *Le Pontifical Romain au Moyen Age III. Le Pontifical de Guillaume Durand*, Studi e Testi 88 (Vatican City: Biblioteca Apostolica Vaticana, 1940).

9. William Durand, *Guillelmi Duranti Rationale divinorum officiorum*, ed. Anselme Davril and Timothy M. Thibodeau, Corpus Christianorum, Continuatio Mediaevalis 140, 140A, 140B (Turnhout: Brepols Publishers, 1995–2000).

10. Daniel Waley, *The Papal State in the Thirteenth Century* (London: Macmillan, 1961), remains a classic account of the religious and political upheavals of Italy during Durand's career.

11. A transcription of the text can be found in Vincenzo Forcella, *Iscrizioni delle Chiesi e d'Altri Edifici di Roma* (Rome: Tip. delle scienze matematiche e fisiche, 1869), 1:411. It is quite likely that this epitaph was composed by his nephew, William Durand the Younger (d. 1330), who became the next bishop of Mende.

12. Standard works on the subject of *Expositiones Missae* are: Joseph Jungmann, *The Mass of the Roman Rite: Its Origins and Development*, trans. Francis A. Brunner, 2 vols. (Westminster, Md.: Christian Classics, 1951–1955; repr., 1986); Roger E. Reynolds, "Liturgy, Treatises on," *Dictionary of the Middle Ages* 7 (1986): 624–33; Cyrille Vogel, *Medieval Liturgy: An Introduction to the Sources*, trans. and rev. W. G. Storey and N. K. Rasmussen (Washington, D.C.: The Pastoral Press, 1986).

13. Prosper Guéranger, *Institutions Liturgiques* (Paris: Débécourt, 1840), 1:355.

14. For an excellent compendium of introductory essays on virtually all of these topics, see Thomas J. Heffernan and E. Ann Matter, eds., *The Liturgy of the Medieval Church* (Kalamazoo, Mich.: Medieval Institute Publications, 2001).

15. I have discussed at length the relationship between the religious and architectural changes of the Gothic Age and liturgical commentary in "Western Christendom," in *The Oxford History of Christian Worship*, ed. Geoffrey Wainwright and Karen B. Westerfield Tucker (Oxford: Oxford University Press, 2006), 216–53.

16. A brilliant analysis of the intellectual, social, and cultural currents of this era can be found in Georges Duby, *The Age of the Cathedrals: Art and Society, 980–1420*, trans. Eleanor Levieux and Barbara Thompson (Chicago: University of Chicago Press, 1981). A detailed presentation of the most recent scholarship on this subject can be found in Elizabeth C. Parker, "Architecture as Liturgical Setting," in *The Liturgy of the Medieval Church*, ed. Thomas J. Heffernan and E. Anne Matter (Kalamazoo, Mich.: Medieval Institute Publications, 2001), 273–326.

17. Honorius Augustodunensis, *Gemma animae, PL* 172:41–738; *Sacramentarium seu de causis et significatu mystico rituum divini in Ecclesia officii liber, PL* 172:737–806. Though this prolific author was referred to as "Honorius Augustodunensis," or from Autun, modern scholars have been unable to determine his place of origin.

18. Pseudo-Hugh of St. Victor, *Speculum de mysteriis Ecclesiae, PL* 177:335–80. This anonymous work, which was attributed to the spiritual master Hugh of St. Victor (d. 1142), was one of Durand's favorite sources in the composition of book 1.

19. Sicardus of Cremona, *Mitrale seu de ecclesiasticis officiis summa, PL* 213:13–434. Before the publication of the *Rationale*, Sicardus' commentary was by far the lengthiest and most extensive medieval treatise on the liturgy. Divided into nine books, it was the basis for a substantial portion of Durand's own text, often presented verbatim throughout the first seven books of the *Rationale*.

20. I .M. Hanssens, ed., *Amalarii episcopi opera liturgica omnia*, Studi e Testi 138–140 (Vatican City: Biblioteca Apostolica Vaticana, 1948–1950).

21. Jungmann, *The Mass of the Roman Rite*, 1:87–92.

22. William Durand, *Rationale*, Prohemium.10, *CCCM* 140:7. I have discussed the relation between allegorical biblical exegesis and liturgical commentary in Timothy M. Thibodeau, *"Enigmata Figurarum*: Biblicial Exegesis and Liturgical Exposition in Durand's *Rationale,"* *Harvard Theological Review* 86 (1993): 65–79. Durand stood in the well-established tradition that employed "four senses" of biblical interpretation (historical, allegorical, tropological, anagogical). The definitive study of medieval biblical commentary is Henri de Lubac, *Exégèse médiévale: Les quatre sens de l'Écriture*, 2 vols. in 4 parts (Paris: Aubier, 1959–1964).

23. Durand, *Rationale*, 8.14, *CCCM* 140B:174.

24. I have discussed this topic in Timothy M. Thibodeau, "The Influence of Canon Law on Liturgical Exposition, c. 1100–1300," *Sacris Erudiri* 37 (1997): 185–202.

25. Isidore of Seville, *Isidorus Hispalensis, Etymologiarum sive originum libri xx*, ed. W. M. Lindsay (Oxford: Oxford University Press, 1911; repr., New York: Oxford University Press, 1990).

26. John Beleth, *Iohannis Beleth Summa de ecclesiasticis officiis*, ed. Herbert Douteil, Corpus Christianorum, Continuatio Mediaevalis 41–41A (Turnhout: Brepols Publishers, 1976).

27. Durand, *Rationale*, 1.5.15, *CCCM* 140:62.

28. I have offered an extensive analysis of this chapter in Timothy M. Thibodeau, "Canon Law and Liturgical Exposition in Durand's *Rationale,"* *Bulletin of Medieval Canon Law* 22 (1998): 41–52. For a historical presentation and analysis of the dedication rite in the Roman pontificals, see Nancy Spatz, "Church Porches and the Liturgy in Twelfth-Century Rome," in *The Liturgy of the Medieval Church*, ed. Thomas J. Heffernan and E. Anne Matter (Kalamazoo, Mich.: Medieval Institute Publications, 2001), 327–367.

29. For the definitive analysis of the early printed editions of the *Rationale*, see Michel Albaric, "Les Éditions imprimées du *Rationale divinorum officiorum* de Guillaume Durand de Mende," in *Guillaume Durand, Évêque de Mende (v. 1230–1296): Canoniste, liturgiste et homme politique*, ed. Pierre-Marie Gy, O.P. (Paris: Éditions du Centre National de la Recherche Scientifique, 1992), 183–200; and Bertrand Guyot, "Essai de classement des editions du *Rationale,"* in *Guillaume Durand, Évêque de Mende (v. 1230–1296): Canoniste, liturgiste et homme politique*, ed. Pierre-Marie Gy, O.P. (Paris: Éditions du Centre National de la Recherche Scientifique, 1992), 201–5.

30. Clarence C. Ménard, "William Durand's *Rationale divinorum officiorum*. Preliminaries to a New Critical Edition" (Ph.D. diss, Gregorian University, 1967).

31. Our critical edition prints the text of the first redaction in large type; where there is an addition to the text from the second redaction, that new text is printed in smaller characters so that the reader may distinguish between the two versions. My translation presents the text as it existed in its final form (i.e., the second redaction).

32. A modern partial edition was done by J. P. Williman, *"Le racional de Divins Offices: An Introduction and Partial Edition"* (Ph.D. diss., University of North Carolina, 1967). A new critical edition of Golein's translation is being prepared by Professors Charles Brucker and Pierre Demarolle.

33. G. H. Buijssen, ed., *Durandus' Rationale in spätmittelhochdeutscher Übersetzung*, 4 vols. (Assen: Van Gorcum, 1966–1983).

34. Charles Barthélemy, *Rational ou Manuel des divins offices de Guillaume Durand, Évêque de Mende au treizième siècle, ou Raisons mystiques et historiques de la liturgie Catholique*, 5 vols. (Paris: Louis Vivès 1854). The title page identifies Barthélemy as, "Membre de la Société des Antiquaires de Picardie, Correspondent du Ministère de l'Instruction publique pour les Travaux historiques."

35. Barthélemy, *Rational*, vii: "L'étude consciencieuse de ces temps de foi et génie nous a fait sentir le vide qui existe dans nos âmes."

36. Most of the modern printed editions rely, in one form or another, on the 1551 edition of Nicholas Doard, a cleric from Champagne, who "corrected" and "annotated" an Italian text-type edition of the *Rationale* (which largely amounts to his production of interpolations into the original text).

37. For the historical and religious context of Neale's work, see A. G. Lough, *John Mason Neale: Priest Extraordinary* (Devon: A. G. Lough, 1975), and Kenneth Hylson-Smith, *High Churchmanship in the Church of England* (Edinburgh: T and T Clark, 1993).

38. John Mason Neale and Benjamin Webb, *The Symbolism of Churches and Church Ornaments: A Translation of the First Book of the Rationale Divinorum Officiorum Written by William Durandus* (Leeds: T.W. Green, 1843).

39. Ibid., xiv.

40. The first passage involves the conjugal duty of husband and wife; in omitting this paragraph, Neale states in a footnote, "A few passages have been omitted in the course of this chapter." The second passage is a citation from Pseudo-Jerome, found in the *Decretum* (c. 1140) of the canonist Gratian, explaining why the Holy Spirit is not present during the conjugal act.

41. The biblical citiations are collated to the critical edition of the Vulgate edited by Robert Weber and Boniface Fischer, *Biblia Sacra iuxta Vulgatam Versionem*, 3rd ed. (Stuttgart: Deutsche Bibelgesellschaft, 1983). The abbreviations for the biblical books conform to *The Holy Bible New Revised Standard Version, Catholic Edition* (Oxford and New York: Oxford University Press, 1999).

PROLOGUE

1. Dig. 1.3.20, Mommsen 1:34.

2. The term Durand uses is *ornamentis*. In some instances I have translated this word as "furnishings," when, for example, he makes generic references to the objects that are typically found in a church. In this case I have used the term "ornament" because of his specificity; that is, he says that he will explain each of these items as individual ornaments used for liturgical rituals.

3. *Rationale*, 4.42.25.

4. Durand uses a common generic term in Latin to describe the formal liturgies of the Church, including the Mass and the Liturgy of the Hours recited communally by monastic and cathedral clergy.

5. Durand has not presented the original text of the Vulgate, hence the garbled nature of this verse: "et isti non cognoverunt vias meas ut iuravi in ira mea si intrabunt in requiem meam" [Ps 94:11, Vulg.].

6. Cf. Dig. 1.2.13, Mommsen 1:30–31.

7. *Rationale*, 5.7.12, Friedberg 2:786.

8. Augustine, *De catechizandis rudibus*, c. 9, *CCSL* 46: 135, cited from D.38 c.11, Friedberg 1:143.

9. *Rationale*, 2.10.14.

10. In keeping with the theological paradigm of medieval Christian writers, Durand believes that Judaism has been invalidated or superseded by the "true" Christian faith. To "Judaize" refers to the danger of Christians lapsing into the outmoded practices of the Judaism of his day.

11. Durand is referring to the prayers that begin the Eucharistic liturgy (i.e., the prayers that precede the *Sanctus* and the Canon of the Mass).

12. Cf. D.6 d.p.c.3, Friedberg 1:11.

13. Ibid.

14. Boethius, *De fide Catholica*, ed. H. F. Stewart and E. K. Rand (Cambridge, Mass.: Harvard University Press, 1978), 58.

15. Jerome, *Comment. in Amos*, 2.4, CCSL 76:261–62.

16. I am obviously aware that Durand's transliterations of Greek terms are imprecise and sometimes incorrect. I have generally preserved his spellings and only made corrections in the most egregious cases.

17. Cf. Isidore, *Etym.*, 1.27.22.

18. Ibid.

19. *Rationale*, 6.81.1 et seq.

20. As a trained canon lawyer, Durand undoubtedly has in mind legal proceedings in this rather awkward passage.

21. This Pseudo-Augustinian text comes from D.11 c.5, Friedberg 1:24. It is actually a Latin translation of a passage from Basil, *De Spiritui Sancto*, 27.66, *PG* 32:187A.

22. Durand is, of course, referring to his mammoth textbook on procedural law. This paragraph parallels his introduction to the previous work, *Speculum iudiciale*, Proem.26.5 (Basel: Froben, 1574; reprint, Darmstadt: Aalen 1975), 5.

23. Augustine, *Ad inquisitiones Ianuarii*, Ep. 55.35, CSEL 34.2:210; cited from D.12 c.12, Friedberg 1:134.

24. D.36 c.2, Friedberg 1:134; cf. Ex 28:15–30, where the breastplate is described. In Jerome's Vulgate translation of the Bible it is called the *Rationale iudicii*. According to the biblical text, the breastplate had a pouch that contained two stones, the *Urim* and *Thummim*, Hebrew terms of uncertain origin that Jerome translated as *doctrina* and *veritas* (doctrine and truth). The stones seem to have been employed for some ritual to determine God's judgment for the Israelites.

1. ON THE CHURCH BUILDING AND ITS PARTS

1. In my translation, I have made a distinction between Durand's two uses of the word *ecclesia*. The lowercase spelling (church) is reserved for the generic church building, while the uppercase (Church) applies to the universal Church, or body of believers.

2. *Rationale*, 1.6.1 et seq.

3. Isidore, *Etym.*, 8.1.7–8.

4. Isidore, *Etym.* 8.1.5–6.

5. Jerome, *Liber interpret. Hebraic. Nominum*, Litt I., CCSL 72:121.

6. *Rationale*, 1.6.5.

7. *Rationale*, 1.2.4.

8. *Rationale*, 2.10.8.

9. *Rationale*, 4.1.13.

10. Continuing with his military metaphors, Durand undoubtedly is referring to the

Roman practice of the victorious general celebrating a "triumph," or a military parade through the streets of Rome.

11. Antiphon at Lauds, for the Dedication of a Church: *CAO* 1680, Hesbert 3:83.
12. De cons. D.1 c.9, Friedberg 1:1296.
13. *Rationale*, 5.2.57.
14. Durand refers to a wood that is also called *shittim* in Hebrew, out of which the Ark and parts of the Tabernacle were constructed. Durand uses the Latin transliteration, *sethim*.
15. Petrus Comestor, *Historia Scholastica*, Lib. Exod. c.45, *PL* 198:1169D–1170A.
16. "[C]rux ex utraque parte;" what Durand means here is the cruciform structure of the building itself, not a processional or liturgical cross.
17. Durand misattributes this passage to Richard when, in fact, it comes from Hugh of St. Victor, *Sermones centum*, c. 1, *PL* 177:902B. His source for this error is Jacob of Voragine, *Jacobi a Voragine Legenda Aurea, vulgo Historia Lombardia dicta*, c. 181.4, ed. Theodore Graesse (Dresden and Leipzig: Arnold, 1846), 837.
18. Isidore, *Etym.*, 6.19.5; Isidore, *Liber de eccles. offic.*, 1.2, *CCSL* 113:5.
19. Jacob of Voragine, *Legenda aurea*, c. 181.4, 837; Cassiodorus, *Historia eccles. tripart.*, 10.9, *CSEL* 71: 596.
20. *Rationale*, 4.5.1.
21. *Rationale*, 4.6.1.
22. Isidore, *Eytm.*, 6.19.6.
23. Cf. Jerome, *Comment. in Matth.*, 1.2, *CCSL* 76:449.
24. "[R]ectum representat predicantis sermonem"; this could also be translated as "ortho-dox" or "morally correct" teaching of the preacher.
25. Durand is referring to the *titulus*, or the inscription placed, at the order of Pilate, on the top of Christ's cross which proclaimed him: "Jesus of Nazareth, King of the Jews."
26. "[P]orta a portando quia per eam portantur quecumque efferuntur."
27. *Rationale*, 6.2.15.
28. *Rationale*, 1.3.28.
29. *Rationale*, 1.3.35.
30. *Rationale*, 4.24.17.
31. *Rationale*, 2.11.2.
32. *Rationale*, 2.7.1.
33. "[D]e medio corde redemptorem nostrum diligimus"; literally "from the middle of our heart."
34. *Ave salus totius seculi arbor salutifera*; this otherwise unknown text was found by Durand in (Ps.-)Hugh of St. Victor, *Speculum de mysteriis ecclesiae*, c. 1, *PL* 177:337D.
35. "[Q]ui ut seruum redimeret tradidit unicum filium"; a paraphrase of the text of the *Exsultet*, Sp 1022a, Deshusses 1:361. This hymn is sung by the deacon when the Paschal candle is lit on Holy Saturday.
36. *Rationale*, 1.6.27.
37. *Rationale*, 1.3.5.
38. Sicardus of Cremona, *Mitrale seu de ecclesiasticis officiis summa*, 1.4, *PL* 213:25A.
39. X 3.1.1, Friedberg 2:449.
40. By "servitium Dei," Durand means the Divine Office or liturgy of the hours.
41. "Diversitas autem officinarum"; literally, "the diversity of workshops."
42. *Rationale*, 5.5.3. Prime is a liturgical office of communal morning prayer.
43. *Rationale*, 2.1.24.
44. *Rationale*, 5.1.1 et seq.

45. Bede, *In Lucam*, 1.2.43–35, *CCSL* 120:72.
46. John Chrysostom, *Hom. in Epist. ad Hebraeos*, 9.15, *PG* 63:339; cited in Sicardus, *Mitrale*, 1.11, *PL* 213:38B.
47. Cf. X 3.49.9, Friedberg 2:657.
48. De cons. D.1 c.36, Friedberg 1:1303.
49. *Rationale*, 5.1.11–16.

2. ON THE ALTAR

1. Isidore, *Etym.*, 15.4.14.
2. From the Canon of the Mass, H 13, Deshusses 1:90. Durand does not provide a complete citation, but I have translated that line of the Canon in full for the sake of clarity.
3. *Rationale*, 6.76.2.
4. *Rationale*, 4.1.15.
5. Isidore, *Etym.*, 6.19.35.
6. Isidore, *Etym.*, 15.14.5.
7. "[R]egularis vita;" this can be literally translated as "regular life," which for a medieval author refers explicitly to the professed religious who live by a formal rule.
8. Durand's presentation is a substantially rewritten paraphrase of the Vulgate text, which reads, in part: "gustavit quia bona est negotiatio eius, non extinguetur in nocte lucerna illius" [Prov 31:18].
9. *Rationale*, 1.23.3.
10. Gregory the Great, *Homelia in Evang.*, 1.7, *PL* 76:1103A.
11. *Rationale*, 1.7.18.
12. Bernard of Clairvaux, *De Consideratione*, 2.7, ed. J. Leclercq and H. Rochais (Rome: Editiones Cisterciensis,1963) 3:422. Durand does not quote Bernard directly, but cites a paraphrase from Jacob of Voragine's *Golden Legend*.
13. *Rationale*, 4.23.1–2.
14. *Liber Pont.*, c. 8, Duchesne 1:128.
15. Gregory the Great, *Regula Pastoralis*, 3.9, *SC* 382:298.
16. "[C]olumnas eius fecit argenteas reclinatorium aureum ascensum purpureum" [Cant. 3:10].
17. Psalms 119–133 (Vulgate numbering) or 120–133 (Hebrew numbering). Biblical scholars note that these "Psalms of ascent" may have originally been part of a pilgrimage ritual to Jerusalem among the ancient Israelites. They came to be known in the medieval Church as the Fifteen Gradual Psalms, from the Latin term for them as "songs of the steps," *canticum graduum.*
18. C.26 q.5 c.13, Friedberg 1:1031–32.
19. VI 1.16.2, Friedberg 2:986.
20. De cons. D.1 c.26, Friedberg 1:1300–1301.

3. ON THE PICTURES, CURTAINS, AND ORNAMENTS OF THE CHURCH

1. Gregory the Great, *Registrum Epist.*, 9.209, *CCSL* 140A:768; cited from De cons. D.3 c.27, Friedberg 1:1360.
2. The Latin text of this verse can be found in Ulysses Chevalier, *Repertorium Hymnologicum*, vol. 3, n. 2600 (Louvain: Polleunis & Ceuterick, 1904), 190.

3. Gregory the Great, *Regula Pastoralis*, 2.10, *SC* 381:242.
4. *Rationale*, 4.39.2.
5. De cons. D.3 c.9, Friedberg 1:1354–55.
6. Gregory the Great, *Registrum Epist.*, 9.209, *CCSL* 140A:768.
7. *Rationale*, 1.1.2 et seq.
8. De cons. D.3 c.29, Friedberg 1:1360.
9. *Rationale*, 7.4.44.
10. *Rationale*, 7.4.44.
11. *Rationale*, 7.25.2; 7.38.1.
12. *Rationale*, 7.44.6.
13. *AMS* 118a, Hesbert 3:132–33. The text is Psalm 91:13, used as the Introit for the Vigil of the Evangelists.
14. Gregory the Great, *Registrum Epist.*, 1.24, 6.63, *CCSL* 40:23, 438.
15. Cf. *AMS* 114, 148a, Hesbert 3:130–31; Introit or Offertory for the Common of Martyrs.
16. *CAO* 2877, Hesbert 3:228; Antiphon for the Saints in the Time of Easter.
17. Cf. John the Deacon, *Vita Gregorii*, 4.84, *PL* 75:231A.
18. *Rationale*, 4.17.2.
19. *Rationale*, 3.17.14.
20. *Rationale*, 8.4.2 sq.
21. Horace, *De Arte Poetica*, ed. F. Vollmer (Leipzig: Teubner, 1929), 226.
22. Cf. Jerome, *Comment. in Esaiam*, 18.65.4–5, *CCSL* 73A:746–48.
23. This is not a correct transliteration of the Greek, φιλέω, to "love or be fond of."
24. There is no such word in Greek, as Durand presents it in Latin transliteration. He must mean *termon*, from the Greek, τέρμων, for "boundary."
25. *Rationale*, 1.2.4.
26. *Rationale*, 1.2.12.
27. *Rationale*, 4.1.13.
28. *Rationale*, 4.6.3–5.
29. Though Durand presents it as such, this not a direct quotation but rather a substantially altered paraphrase of the text of the Vulgate.
30. *Rationale*, 3.19.14.
31. *Rationale*, 4.35.3.
32. *Rationale*, 4.1.13.
33. This is an obscure passage in Latin; it is not clear what the precise meaning of this term is for Durand. It could simply refer to a choir that is elevated above the pavement of the church floor, hence his reference to the people being able to see the choir singing.
34. By "feasts with nine lessons," Durand means liturgical celebrations that have nine biblical readings and Psalms.
35. C.33 q.4 c.9, Friedberg 1:1249.
36. Burchard of Worms, *Decretum*, 13.10, *PL* 140:886D.
37. *Rationale*, 6.77.1.
38. *Rationale*, 1.2.7.
39. Here the word *thesaurus* or "treasury" means the room where sacred relics and other precious objects were stored under lock and key.
40. Durand may also be alluding to the Antiphon for the Nativity or Assumption of the B.V.M., *CAO* 3878, Hesbert 3:349.

41. This may also be allusion to the Antiphon for the Dedication of a Church, *CAO* 2341, Hesbert 3:164.
42. *Rationale*, 6.86.15.
43. *Rationale*, 6.72.1.
44. "[R]espexit Deus Petrum postquam negavit Christum." I have corrected Durand's "Deus" to "Dominus" in the translation.
45. *Liber Pont.*, c. 16, Duchesne 1:139.
46. *Liber Pont.*, c. 18, Duschesne 1:143.
47. De cons. D.1 c. 45, Friedberg 1:1306.
48. Durand has altered the Vulgate version of this Psalm, "calix in manu Domini," the chalice in the Lord's hand.
49. *Rationale*, 1.8.24.
50. *Rationale*, 1.1.12.
51. *Rationale*, 3.19.1, 17.
52. *Rationale*, 1.6.1.
53. De cons. D.1 c.43, Friedberg 1:1305.
54. De cons. D.1 c.42, Friedberg 1:1305.
55. Durand is referring to Daniel 5:1–4, where the sacred objects plundered from Solomon's Temple in Jerusalem by the Babylonian king Nebuchadnezzar were desecrated by his successor Belshazzar during a dinner party. A coded message then appeared on the wall that was interpreted by Daniel to signal the swift death of the king and the Persian conquest of his kingdom.
56. De cons. D.1 c.40, Friedberg 1:1304.
57. De cons. D.4 c.106, Friedberg 1:1395.
58. De cons. D.1 c.39, Friedberg 1:1303–04.
59. *Rationale*, 1.8.27.

4. ON THE BELLS

1. *Rationale*, 6.107.11.
2. Gregory the Great, *Regula Pastoralis*, 2.4, *SC* 381:190, cited from D.43 c.1, Friedberg 1:154.
3. Though presented as such, this is not a direct citation of 2 Cor. 5:13, but more of a paraphrase.
4. Cf. Gregory the Great, *Regula Pastoralis*, 3.4, *SC* 382:508.
5. *Liber Pont.*, c. 67, Duchesne 1:315.
6. From the Latin word for "seventieth," even though this liturgical period is not seventy days in length. It was the ninth Sunday before Easter and the third Sunday before Lent in the medieval Roman calendar. Purple vestments were worn by the priest or bishop at Mass until Holy Week, and "Alleluia" would not be sung during Mass.
7. "[I]n profestis diebus"; Church feasts that are not considered "holidays."
8. *Rationale*, 5.3.30.
9. Durand means, for example, that it would be rung more times for a priest or bishop than an acolyte or subdeacon.
10. *Rationale*, 4.6.19.
11. *Rationale*, 6.72.3, 6.72.5.
12. A reference to the medieval canonical practice of prohibiting the celebration of the

liturgy or reception of the sacraments for a local church or region which had incurred the censure of the Church.

13. *Rationale*, 4.34.10.

5. ON THE CEMETERY AND OTHER SACRED AND RELIGIOUS PLACES

1. Although Durand does not name him, the etymologies of this chapter are derived almost entirely from John Beleth, *Summa de ecclesiasticis officiis*, ed. H. Douteil, *CCCM* 41A (Turnhout: Brepols, 1976). Beleth himself often relied on Isidore of Seville's famous *Etymologiae*. Much of that Isidorean material becomes part of Durand's presentation.

2. *Rationale*, 1.1.2.

3. C.17 q.4 c.7, Friedberg 1:816.

4. By being "received," Durand means that the inhabitants of that particular place formally give someone sanctuary.

5. Inst. 2.1.10, Mommsen 1:10.

6. Dig. 11.7.44, Mommsen 1:190.

7. Oddly, even as he disputes the validity of Roman civil law on this point, Durand cites no text from canon law to support his argument.

8. Isidore, *Etym.*, 15.11.3. This is a reference to a fourth-century B.C. ruler of Caria, who was married to her own brother, Mausolus, and was grief-stricken at his death in 353 B.C.

9. Isidore, *Etym.*, 15.11.1–2.

10. A reference to the Ash Wednesday Liturgy; the Latin text is from the *Ordinarium Innocentii III*, in the *OrdPC*, 178, no. 3.

11. Isidore, *Etym.*, 15.6.1.

12. Isidore, *Etym.*, 15.11.2.

13. Cf. Isidore, *Etym.*, 15.11.4.

14. I have been unable to identify Durand's source for this obscure reference.

15. Cf. Suetonius, *De vita Caesarum*, 1.85, ed. M. Ihm (Leipzig: Teubner, 1925), 43–44.0

16. Jerome, *Hebraic. quaest. in libro Genesos*, CCSL 72: 40–56; cited in C.13 q.2 c.2, Friedberg 1:721.

17. X 3.28.12, Friedberg 2:553.

18. Gregory the Great, *Dialogi*, 4.54, SC 165:180.

19. Gregory the Great, *Dialogi*, 4.56, SC 265:182–84.

20. C.13 q.2 c.16, Friedberg 1:726; in the *Decretum*, from which Durand cites it, this text is attributed to Saint Augustine, when in fact, it comes from Gregory the Great, *Dialogi*, 4.52, SC 265:176.

21. Augustine, *De cura pro mortuis gerenda*, 18.22, CSEL 41:659; cited from C.13 q.2 c.19, Friedberg 1:727.

22. De cons. D.14 c.35, Friedberg 1:1374.

23. C.13 q.2 c.18, Friedberg 1:727.

24. *Rationale*, 7.35.36 et seq.

6. ON THE DEDICATION OF A CHURCH

1. *Rationale*, 7.48.1.

2. Burchard of Worms, *Decretum*, 3.58, PL 140: 684C–685C; De cons. D.1 c.2, Friedberg 1:1293–94.

3. Cf. *Liber Pont.*, c. 56, Duchesne 1:279.
4. I have been unable to identify Durand's obscure reference.
5. C.26 q.6 c.2, Friedberg 1:1036; X 3.40.9, Friedberg 2:635.
6. Jacob of Voragine, *Legenda aurea*, c. 182, ed. Theodore Graesse (Dresden and Leipzig: Arnold, 1846), 854.
7. De cons. D.1 c.10, Friedberg 1:1296; cf. X 3.28.12, Friedberg 2:553.
8. De cons. D.4 cc.114–15, Friedberg 1:1397.
9. X 3.40.5, Friedberg 2:634; cf. *PGD* 2.2.1, Andrieu 3:455.
10. Gregory the Great, *Dialogi*, 3.30, SC 260:378–84.
11. Cf. C.23 q.5 c.7, Friedberg 1:932.
12. Collect from the Mass for the Dedication of a Church; H 817, Deshusses 1:304.
13. *Rationale*, 1.1.4.
14. The rubrics and prayer texts in this paragraph come from the *Ordines Romani* and Durand's own *Pontifical*. See *Ordo* 41.2.2–7, OR 4:339–40; *PGD* 2.2.28, 2.2.32, 2.2.36, 2.2.39: 460–62.
15. In 609, Pope Boniface IV (r. 608–615) dedicated the Roman pagan temple known as Hadrian's Pantheon, turning it into a Christian Church, in honor of the Blessed Virgin Mary and all Martyrs (*Sancta Maria ad Martyres*). The date of the Feast was May 13.
16. *Rationale*, 1.7.4 et seq..
17. Prayer for the exorcism of water; H 985, Deshusses 1:336–37.
18. In this tortuous phrase, Durand makes an allusion to the story of Adam and Eve being deceived by the Devil into eating the forbidden fruit in the Garden of Eden.
19. *Rationale*, 1.1.14.
20. From the rite for the Dedication of a Church, *PGD*, 2.2.28; 2.2.32: 460, 461.
21. Hymn for the Vigil of Ascension, *Aeterne Rex Altissime*, *AHMA*, no. 39, vol. 27:96.
22. Durand cites an unidentified text.
23. *PGD*, 2.2.39: 462.
24. Much of the nuance and double entendre of Durand's Latin cannot survive in translation. When he speaks of the Jews being "moved to the left," he employs the term *sinister*, which obviously means "the left," but also carries the connation of misfortune or bad luck (*in sinistrum*).
25. *PGD*, 2.2.51: 465.
26. *Ordo* for the blessing of a church: *PCR*, 23.41–42: 431; cf. Mt 21:13.
27. (Ps.-)Bernard of Clairvaux; cited from William of Auxerre, *Summa de Offiiciis Ecclesiasticis*. There is no modern printed edition of this work; I have employed an early-fourteenth-century manuscript of the work (Douai: Bibilothèque municipale, n. 65) for the critical edition of Durand's Latin text.
28. Durand's citation of these popes is incorrect. It should be Gelasius I and Pseudo-Anacletus, as found in Gratian's *Decretum*: D.21 c.3, Friedberg 1: 70; D.22 c.2, Friedberg 1: 73–75.
29. *Rationale*, 1.8.1 et seq.
30. Cf. De cons. D.1 c.20, Friedberg 1:1299; X 3.40.6, Friedberg 2:634.
31. De cons. D.1 c.24, Friedberg 1:1300.
32. De cons. D.1 c.17, Friedberg 1:1298.
33. De cons. D.1 c.19, Friedberg 1:1299; X 3.40.3, Friedberg 2:633.
34. X 3.40.1, Friedberg 2:633.
35. Cf. De cons. D.1 c.19, Friedberg 1:1299.
36. X 3.40.6, Friedberg 2:634.
37. X 3.40.1, Friedberg 2:633.

38. De cons. D.1 c.30, Friedberg 1:301–2; X 5.33.30, Friedberg 2:868–69.
39. The entire paragraph is based on De cons. D.1 c.30, Friedberg 1:1301–2; X 5.33.30, Friedberg 2:868–69.
40. Dig. 39.1.1 §11, Mommsen 1:635.
41. Cf. Dig. 7.1.44, 43.19.1, Mommsen 1:132, 740.
42. By "reconciliation" Durand means the reconsecration of a church that meets the canonical definition of desecration.
43. X 3.40.10, Friedberg 2:635.
44. The remainder of this paragraph is based on X 3.40.4, 7, 9, 10, Friedberg 2:634–35.
45. X 3.40.3, Friedberg 2:633.
46. De cons. D.1 c.19; c.24, Friedberg 1:1299–1300.
47. X 3.49.9, Friedberg 2:635.
48. De cons. D.1 c.33, Friedberg 1:1302; X 3.39.27, Friedberg 2:633.
49. De cons. D.1 c.19, Friedberg 1:1299; X 3.40.10, X 5.16.5, Friedberg 2:635, 806.
50. D.31 c.13, Friedberg 1:114–15.
51. D.6 c.1, Friedberg 1:9.
52. Dig. 9.1.1, Mommsen 1:155; C.15 q.3 c.2, Friedberg 1:751.
53. De cons. D.1 c.c.19–20, Friedberg 1:1299; X 3.40.10, Friedberg 2:635.
54. Cf. Dig. 48.8.17, Mommsen 1:853.
55. C.17 q.4 c.12, Friedberg 1:818.
56. C.17 q.4 c.9, Friedberg 1:817.
57. X 2.28.25, 38, Friedberg 2:417–18.
58. The whole paragraph is based on the following: Dig. 47.12.3 §4, §7, Mommsen 1:837; Dig. 47.12.4, Mommsen 1:837; Dig. 11.7.38, Mommsen 1:189.
59. Cf. X 5.16.5, Friedberg 2:806; X 5.1.27, Friedberg 2:748.
60. X 3.40.4, 3.49.5, Friedberg 2:634, 655.
61. X 3.28.12, 3.40.7, Friedberg 2:553, 634; De cons. D.1 cc.27–28, Friedberg 1:1301–2.
62. *Rationale*, 1.8.1 et seq.
63. X 3.40.7, Friedberg 2:634.
64. C.17 q.4 c.6, c.8, c.10, c.29, Friedberg 1·816–17, 822; X 3.49.5, Friedberg 2:654–57.
65. X 3.40.1, 6, Friedberg 2: 633, 634.
66. Dig. 50.17.35, Mommsen 1:921.
67. De pen. D.1 c.51, Friedberg 1:1170–71.
68. By Pontificals, Durand means the books that regulated the service performed only by a pontiff, or bishop. Cf. *PCR*, 26.1–9: 443–45; *PGD*, 2.7.1–8: 517–18.
69. Cf. C.1 q.1 c.84, C.9 q.1 c.5, Friedberg 1:387–88, 601–2; X 1.16.1–2, X 3.27, Friedberg 2:134, 455–56.
70. *Rationale*, 3.1.1.
71. D.81 c.15, Friedberg 1:284.

7. ON THE DEDICATION OF THE ALTAR

1. De cons. D.1 cc.31–32, Friedberg 1:1302.
2. Durand follows the order presented in his own pontifical: *PGD*, 2.3.11ff.: 481ff.
3. *PGD*, 2.3.10: 480–81.
4. By sepulcher, Durand means the void in the base of the altar where the relics of a particular saint would be permanently housed in a sealed container. On top of this

cavity would sit the "table" of the altar. See *Rationale*, 1.6.34 for a complete discussion of this topic.

5. It is difficult to follow Durand's logic in presenting this passage as some sort of proof text for his argument.
6. *Rationale*, 1.8.3.
7. *Rationale*, 4.4.10.
8. Or to paraphrase, "by frequently making the sign of the cross."
9. Gilbert of Tournai, *Collectio de scandalis Ecclesiae*, 8.2, ed. F. Stroick, *Archivum Franciscanum Historicum* 24 (1931): 41. Durand paraphrases the text composed by the Franciscan Gilbert, whom he heard preach about the scandals afflicting the Church at the Second Council of Lyon (1274).
10. From the prayer for the consecration of an altar: *PGD*, 2.3.16–17: 481–82.
11. From the rite for the blessing of a church: *PCR*, 23.42: 431.
12. *Rationale*, 1.2.4.
13. De cons. D.1 c.26, Friedberg 1:1300–1301; cf. De cons. D.1 c.24, c.30, Friedberg 1:1300, 1301–2.
14. X 3.40.1, Friedberg 2:634.
15. Durand has significantly altered the text of the Vulgate, which reads: "Verumtamen inimicos meos illos qui noluerunt me regnare super se . . . " or, "But even so, my enemies, who did not want me to rule over them. . . . "
16. From the rite for the consecration of an altar: *PGD*, 2.3.43: 487.
17. From the rite for the blessing of a church: *PRS12*, 17.55–57: 188–89.
18. Cited from X 1.15.1, Friedberg 2:132.
19. From the rite for the consecration of an altar: *PGD*, 2.3.51: 489.
20. *PGD*, 2.3.55: 490.
21. This passage is a paraphrase of Gregory the Great, *Homelia in Hiezech. Prophet.*, 6.3–4, *CCSL* 142:69.
22. From the rite for the consecration of an altar: *PGD*, 2.3.70: 493.
23. From the rite for the blessing of a portable altar: *PRG*, 40.27: 169.
24. *Rationale*, 1.2.12.
25. *Rationale*, 4.1.16.
26. "Gelasius" should be "Ignius," as found in De cons. D.1. c.3, Friedberg 1:1294–95.

8. ON CONSECRATIONS AND UNCTIONS

1. This entire paragraph is based on De cons. D.1 c.1–2, Friedberg 1:1293.
2. Paragraph 3 is taken almost entirely from: X 1.15.1, Friedberg 2:131–32.
3. *Rationale*, 6.74.1 et seq..
4. *Rationale*, 1.2.3.
5. Paragraph 5 is taken almost entirely from: D.35 c.2 Friedberg 1:131.
6. Unknown to Durand, this is actually a Pseudo-Augustinian text cited from: D.11 c.5, Friedberg 1:24.
7. *Rationale*, 6.84.3–4.
8. The paragraph can be found nearly verbatim in: X 1.15.1, Friedberg 2:133. The text of Isidore is found in that citation; the original source is Isidore of Seville, *De ecclesiasticis officiis*, 1.1, 2.26, *CCSL* 113:4, 106.
9. *Rationale*, 2.1.4.

10. This Pseudo-Augustinian text is cited from: De cons. D.4 c.73, Friedberg 1:1386–87; Pseduo-Augustine, *Sermo de mysterio baptismatis*, PL 40:1210–12.

11. Rhabanus Maurus, *De institutione clericorum libri tres*, 1.27, ed. A. Knöpfler (Munich: J.J. Lentner'schen Buchhandlung, 1900), 49. Durand cited this text as he found it in: De cons. D.4 c.70, Friedberg 1:1385.

12. Rhabanus, *De instit. cleric.*, 1.28, 1.30, ed. Knöpfler, 51, 53–54. Cited from De cons. D.4 c.88, Friedberg 1:1391; De cons. D.5 c.5, Friedberg 1:1414.

13. *Liber Pont.*, c. 34, Duchesne 1:171; cited from Rhabanus, *De inst. cleric.*, 1.28, ed. Knöpfler, 51.

14. Sicardus, *Mitrale, seu de ecclesiasticis officiis summa*, 6.14, PL 213:333A.

15. Durand is referring to the followers of Arnold of Brescia (c.1100–1154), who was condemned as a heretic by the Council of Sens (1141). Arnold was eventually hanged for his participation in the uprising of the Roman republic (1154); his followers were condemned by the Council of Verona (1184).

16. Rhabanus, *De instit. cleric.*, 1.27, ed. Knöpfler, 49; cited from De cons. D.4 c.70, Friedberg 1:1385.

17. X 1.15.1, Friedberg 2:133.

18. *Rationale*, 6.84.3–4.

19. *Rationale*, 6.84.3.

20. From the prayer for the Ordination of a Priest: *PGD*, 1.13.14, 369; the prayer is also found in C.16 c.1 c.40, Friedberg 1:733; X 1.15.1, Friedberg 2:132.

21. Cf. C.1 q.1 c.47, Friedberg 1:376–77.

22. This sentence and the remainder of this paragraph are taken from: C.23 q.4 c.22, Friedberg 1:906–7.

23. This entire paragraph is taken from: X 1.15.1, Friedberg 2:132.

24. Gregory the Great, *Moralia in Iob*, 2.52, CCSL 143A:109.

25. From the prayer for the Ordination of a Priest: *PGD*, 1.13.14: 369. The prayer is also found in C.16 c.1 c.40, Friedberg 1:733; X 1.15.1, Friedberg 2:132.

26. D.89 c.7, Friedberg 1:313.

27. From the Order for the Consecration of a Bishop: *PCR*, 1.11.30: 363.

28. D.96 c.14, Friedberg 1:342–45; cf. *Liber Pont.*, c. 34, Duchesne 1:172. Durand is citing the so-called Donation of Constantine, in which the emperor bequeathed control of the Western Empire to Pope Sylvester I. The text was proven to be a forgery by the fifteenth-century humanist scholar, Lorenzo Valla.

29. *Rationale*, 2.11.6–7.

30. Virtually all of this paragraph is derived from: X 1.15.1, Friedberg 2:133–34.

31. Cf. *Liber Pont.*, c. 34, Duchesne 1: 171.

32. Burchard of Worms, *Decretum*, 3.58, PL 140:684C–85C.

33. De cons. D.4 c.32, Friedberg 1:1371–72; De cons. D.5 c.1, Friedberg 1:1413.

34. X 5.40.14, Friedberg 2:815.

35. C.26 q.6 cc.10–11, Friedberg 1:1038–39; X 5.39.28, Friedberg 2:899.

36. De cons. D.2 c.97, Friedberg 1:1352.

37. D.5 c.3, Friedberg 1:8.

38. *Rationale*, 6.28.18.

39. Cf. C.17 q.4 cc.20–21, Friedberg 1:819–20; X 3.40.7, Friedberg 2:634.

40. De cons. D.1 cc.27–28, Friedberg 1:1301–2; X 3.28.12, Friedberg 2:553.

41. The beginning of this paragraph is derived from: De cons. D.1 cc.1–2, Friedberg 1:1293–94.

42. D.68 c.4, Friedberg 1:255.
43. Cf. Inst. 2.1.25–26, Mommsen 1:11; X 3.40.3, Friedberg 2:633.
44. *Rationale*, 3.1.1 et seq.
45. *Rationale*, 2.9.10.
46. *Rationale*, 2.1.39 et seq.

9. ON THE ECCLESIASTICAL SACRAMENTS

1. C.1 q.1 c.84, Friedberg 1:388; although attributed to Gregory the Great, the text found in Gratian is a compilation of passages from Isidore of Seville, Jerome, and Gregory. cf. Isidore, *Etym.* 6.19.39.
2. Augustine, *Quaest. et locut. In Hept.*, qu. Lev. 84, *CCSL* 33:228; *De civitate Dei* 10.5, *CCSL* 47:277; cited from De cons. D.2 c.32, Friedberg 1:1324.
3. Augustine, *De doctrina christiana*, 2.1, *CCSL* 32:32; cited from De cons. D.2 c.33, Friedberg 1:1324.
4. *Rationale*, 4.3.30.
5. *Rationale*, 4.42.22.
6. C.1 q.1 c.39, Friedberg 1:374.
7. X 1.1.1 §4, Friedberg 2:5.
8. *Rationale*, 6.82, 6.83 (in full).
9. X 1.4.4, 1.15.1, Friedberg 2:37, 132–33.
10. *Rationale*, 6.84.1 et seq.
11. "[S]ecundum clavis Ecclesie"; literally, "according to the keys of the Church." Durand undoubtedly is alluding to the Papal authority "of binding and loosing," given to St. Peter in the Gospel of Matthew [Mt 16:18–22], symbolized by the "keys to the kingdom of heaven."
12. *Rationale*, 6.84.1.
13. Durand, *Aureum Repertorium super toto corpore iuris canonici*, c. 5 (Venice: Paganinus de Paganinis, 1497), fol. 60v–61v. Durand refers to his own short treatise on Penance, the final version of which was completed c. 1279.
14. *Rationale*, 2.1.4 et seq.
15. This paragraph mirrors Durand's treatment of the Sacrament of Marriage in the synodal statues he published for his diocesan clergy in Mende. See J. Berthelé and M. Valmary, eds. "Les instructions et constitutions de Guillaume Durand le spéculateur, publiées d'après le manuscrit de Cessenon." *Académie des Sciences et Lettres de Montpellier. Mémoires de la Section des Lettres*, 2nd ser., 3 (1905): 45–46.
16. C.1 q.1 d.p.c.39, c. 43, Friedberg 1:374, 375; X 1.1.1 §4, Friedberg 2:5.
17. C.33 q.4 c.8, Friedberg 1:1249; X 2.9.4, Friedberg 2:272.
18. From the Latin word for "seventieth," even though this liturgical period is not seventy days in length. It was the ninth Sunday before Easter and the third Sunday before Lent in the medieval Roman calendar. Purple vestments were worn by the priest or bishop at Mass until Holy Week, and "Alleluia" would not be sung during Mass; hence Durand's reference to this as a "time of sorrow."
19. The Sunday after Easter, called Low Sunday to distinguish it from the great celebration of Easter that precedes it. Durand uses the medieval name, *Dominica in albis depositis*; this refers to newly baptized who removed their white baptismal robes for the first time.
20. Days of prayer and fasting to appease God; from the Latin *rogare*, "to solicit or

entreat." The Major Rogation day was April 25; the Minor Rogations were the three days before the Feast of Ascension (forty days after the celebration of Easter Sunday).

21. X 2.9.4, Friedberg 2:272.

22. C.33 q.4 c.8, Friedberg 1:1249.

23. Durand is referring, of course, to the story of Jesus at the wedding in Cana, where, according to the Gospel narratives, he turned water into wine.

24. An Antiphon and Versicle for the celebration of Epiphany and its Octave, in the Ordinal of Innocent III: *OrdPC*, 145, 151.

25. Most of this paragraph is based on C.33 q.4 cc.1–13, Friedberg 1:1247–50.

26. Cited from X 3.32.3, Friedberg 2:579.

27. C.33 q.4 c.10, Friedberg 1:1249.

28. Durand is referring to Martinmas, or the time surrounding the Feast of St. Martin of Tours (November 11).

29. Isidore of Seville, *De eccles. officiis*, 2.20.68, *CCSL* 113:91–92; cited from C.30 q.5 c.7, Friedberg 1:1106.

30. It is unclear to whom Durand is referring; could it be the mythical Egyptian king mentioned by Herodotus, the Greek historian of the fifth century B.C.?

31. Ambrose, *De Abraham*, 1.9.94, *CSEL* 32.1:563, cited from C.30 q.5 c.8, Friedberg 1:1106.

32. Cited in C.32 q.2 c.4, Friedberg 1:1120–21. This is not Jerome but rather a Latin translation of Origen of Alexandria's *Hom. VI, In Numeros*, c. 3, *PG* 12:610C. Durand's own citation is corrupt and makes little sense as presented in the original Latin. I have corrected the passage in translation, in conformity with the text of Gratian's *Decretum*, which Durand purports to cite.

33. Most of this paragraph is derived from X 1.21.5, Friedberg 2:147–48.

34. Although the word *sacramentum* is employed, in this instance Durand is not using the technical term for "sacrament" but rather a word that is best translated as "mystery" in the Christian sense.

35. D.26 c.2, Friedberg 1:95.

36. This paragraph is based on C.31 q.1 c.8, Friedberg 1:1110; X 4.21.1, 3, Friedberg 2:730, 731.

37. Ibid.

38. C.30 q.5 c.1, Friedberg 1:1104.

39. C.31 q.1 c.8, Friedberg 1:1110; X 4.21.1, 3, Friedberg 2:730, 731.

40. *Rationale*, 2.1.47.

41. *Rationale*, 2.1.39 et seq.

42. De cons. D.2 c.8, Friedberg 1:1317.

43. Jerome, *Ad Rusticum monachum*, Ep. 125.11, *CSEL* 56:130; cited from De cons. D.5 c.33, Friedberg 1:1420–21.

BIBLIOGRAPHY

PRIMARY SOURCES

Andrieu, Michel, ed. *Le Pontifical Romain au Moyen Age II: Le Pontifical de la Curie Romaine*. Studi e Testi 87. Vatican City: Biblioteca Apostolica Vaticana, 1940.

———. *Le Pontifical Romain au Moyen Age III: Le Pontifical de Guillaume Durand*. Studi e Testi 88. Vatican City: Biblioteca Apostolica Vaticana, 1940.

Barthélemy, Charles. *Rational ou Manuel des divins offices de Guillaume Durand, Évêque de Mende au treizième siècle, ou Raisons mystiques et historiques de la liturgie Catholique*. 5 vols. Paris: Loius Vivès, 1854.

Beleth, John. *Iohannis Beleth Summa de ecclesiasticis officiis*. Ed. Herbert Douteil. Corpus Christianorum, Continuatio Mediaevalis 41–41A. Turnhout: Brepols Publishers, 1976.

Bernard of Clairvaux. *De Consideratione*. Ed. J. Leclercq and H. Rochais. Rome: Editiones Cisterciensis, 1963.

Berthelé, J., and M. Valmary, eds. "Les instructions et constitutions de Guillaume Durand le spéculateur, publiées d'après le manuscrit de Cessenon." *Académie des Sciences et Lettres de Montpellier. Mémoires de la Section des Lettres*, 2nd ser., 3 (1905): 1–148.

Boethius. *De fide Catholica*. Ed. H. F. Stewart and E. K. Rand. Cambridge, Mass.: Harvard University Press, 1978.

Buijssen, G. H., ed. *Durandus' Rationale in spätmittelhochdeutscher Übersetzung*. 4 vols. Assen: Van Gorcum, 1966–1983.

Chevalier, Ulysses. *Repertorium Hymnologicum*. 6 vols. Louvain and Brussels, 1892–1921.

Deshusses, Jean, ed. *Le sacramentaire grégorien: Ses principales formes d'après les plus anciens manuscrits*. 2nd ed. Spicilegium Friburgense 16, 24, 28. Fribourg: Éditions universitaires, 1979–1982.

Dreves, G., C. Blume, and H. M. Bannister, eds. *Analecta hymnica medii aevi*. 55 vols. Leipzig: O.R. Reisland, 1886–1922. Indices, ed. Dorothea Baumann. 3 vols. Bern and Munich: Francke, 1978.

Duchesne, Louis. *Le Liber Pontificalis*. 2nd ed. 3 vols. Bibliothèque des Écoles françaises d'Athènes et de Rome. Paris: E. de Boccard, 1955–1957.

Durand, William. *Aureum Repertorium super toto corpore iuris canonici*. Venice: Paganinus de Paganinis, 1497.

———. *In sacrosanctum Lugdunense concilium sub Gregorio X Guilelmi Duranti cognomento Speculatoris commentarius*. Fano: Simone Maiolo, 1569.

————. *Guillelmi Duranti Rationale divinorum officiorum.* Ed. Anselme Davril and Timothy M. Thibodeau. Corpus Christianorum, Continuatio Mediaevalis 140, 140A, 140B. Turnhout: Brepols Publishers, 1995–2000.

————. *Speculum iudiciale, illustratum et repurgatum a Giovanni Andrea et Baldo degli Ubaldi.* 4 parts in 2 vols. Basel: Froben, 1574. Reprint, Darmstadt: Aalen, 1975.

Friedberg, Emile. *Corpus Iuris Canonici.* 2 vols. Leipzig: Bernard Tauchnitz, 1879. Reprint, Graz: Akademische Druck-u. Verlagsanstalt, 1959.

Gilbert of Tournai. *Collectio de scandalis Ecclesiae.* Ed. F. Stroick. *Archivum Franciscanum Historicum* 24 (1931): 33–62.

Hanssens, I. M., ed. *Amalarii episcopi opera liturgica omnia.* Studi e Testi 138–140. Vatican City: Bibiloteca Apostolica Vaticana, 1948–1950.

Hesbert, René J.. *Corpus antiphonalium officii.* 6 vols. and indices. Rome: Herder, 1963–1979.

————. *Antiphonale Missarum Sextuplex.* Bruselles: Vromant, 1935.

Honorius Augustodunensis. *Gemma animae.* PL 172:541–738.

————. *Sacramentarium seu de causis et significatu mystico rituum divini in Ecclesia officii liber.* PL 172:813–1108.

Horace. *De Arte Poetica.* Ed. F. Vollmer. Leipzig: Teubner, 1929.

Pseudo-Hugh of St. Victor. *Speculum de mysteriis ecclesiae.* PL 177:335–80.

Isidore of Seville. *Isidorus Hispalensis Etymologiarum sive originum libri xx.* Ed. W. M. Lindsay. Oxford: Oxford University Press, 1911. Reprint, New York: Oxford University Press, 1990.

————. *Sancti Isidori Episcopi Hispalensis De ecclesiasticis officiis.* Edited by C. M. Lawson. Corpus Christianorum, Series Latina 113. Turnhout: Brepols Publishers,1989.

Jacob of Voragine. *Jacobi a Voragine Legenda Aurea, vulgo Historia Lombardia dicta.* Ed. Theodore Graesse. Dresden and Leipzig: Arnold, 1846.

Mommsen, Theodore, et al. *Corpus Iuris Civilis.* 3 vols. Berlin: Weidmann, 1872–1895. Reprint, Hildesheim: Weidmann, 1988–1989.

Rhabanus Maurus. *Rabani Mauri De institutione clericorum libri tres.* Ed. Aloisius Knöpfler. Munich: J.J. Lentner'schen Buchhandlung, 1900.

Neale, John Mason, and Benjamin Webb. *The Symbolism of Churches and Church Ornaments: A Translation of the First Book of the Rationale Divinorum Officiorum Written by William Durandus.* Leeds: T. W. Green, 1843.

Sicardus of Cremona. *Mitrale seu de ecclesiasticis officiis summa.* PL 213:13–434.

Suetonius. *De vita Caesarum.* Ed. M. Ihm. Leipzig: Teubner, 1925.

Van Dijk, S.J.P., and Joan Hazeldon Walker, eds. *The Ordinal of the Papal Court from Innocent III to Boniface VIII and Related Documents.* Spicilegium Friburgense 22. Fribourg: University Press, 1975.

Vogel, C., and R. Elze. *Le Pontifical romano-germanique du Xe siècle.* Studi e Testi 226, 227, 269. Vatican City: Bibiloteca Apostolica Vaticana, 1963–1972.

Weber, Robert, and Boniface Fischer, eds. *Biblia Sacra iuxta Vulgatam Versionem.* 3rd ed. Stuttgart: Deutsche Bibelgesellschaft, 1983.

SECONDARY SOURCES

Albaric, Michel. "Les Éditions imprimées du *Rationale divinorum officiorum* de Guillaume Durand de Mende." In *Guillaume Durand, Évêque de Mende (v. 1230–1296): Canoniste, liturgiste et homme politique*, ed. Pierre-Marie Gy, O.P., 183–200. Paris: Éditions du Centre National de la Recherche Scientifique, 1992.

Duby, Georges. *The Age of the Cathedrals: Art and Society, 980–1420*. Trans. Eleanor Levieux and Barbara Thompson. Chicago: University of Chicago Press, 1981.

Faletti, Louis. "Guillaume Durand." *Dictionnaire de droit canonique* 5 (1953): 1014–75.

Faupel-Drevs, Kirstin. *Vom rechten Gebrauch der Bilder im liturgischen Raum: mittelalterliche Funktionsbestimmungen bildender Kunst im Rational divinorum officiorum des Durandus von Mende, 1230–1296*. Leiden: Brill, 2000.

Forcella, Vincenzo. *Iscrizioni delle Chiesi e d'Altri Edifici di Roma*. Rome: Tip. delle scienze matematiche e fisiche, 1869.

Gimpel, Jean. *The Cathedral Builders*. Trans. Teresa Waugh. New York: Grove Press, 1983.

Guéranger, Prosper. *Institutions liturgiques*. Paris: Débécourt, 1840.

Guyot, Bertrand. "Essai de classement des editions du *Rationale*." In *Guillaume Durand, Évêque de Mende (v. 1230–1296): Canoniste, liturgiste et homme politique*, ed. Pierre-Marie Gy, O.P., 201–5. Paris: Éditions du Centre National de la Recherche Scientifique, 1992.

Gy, Pierre-Marie, O.P., ed. *Guillaume Durand, Évêque de Mende (v. 1230–1296): Canoniste, liturgiste et homme politique*. Paris: Éditions du Centre National de la Recherche Scientifique, 1992.

———. "L'Ordinaire de Mende, une oeuvre inédite de Guillaume Durand l'Ancien." *Cahiers de Fanjeaux* 17 (1982): 239–49.

Harper, John. *The Forms and Orders of the Western Liturgy from the Tenth to the Eighteenth Century: A Historical Introduction and Guide for Students and Musicians*. Oxford: Oxford University Press, 1991.

Heffernan, Thomas J., and E. Ann Matter. *The Liturgy of the Medieval Church*. Kalamazoo, Mich.: Medieval Institute Publications, 2001.

Hylson-Smith, Kenneth. *High Churchmanship in the Church of England*. Edinburgh: T and T Clark, 1993.

Jungmann, Joseph A. *The Mass of the Roman Rite: Its Origins and Development*. Trans. Francis A. Brunner. 2 vols. Westminster, Md.: Christian Classics, 1951–1955; reprint, 1986.

Klauser, Theodor. *A Short History of the Western Liturgy: An Account and Some Reflections*. 2nd ed. Trans. John Halliburton. Oxford: Oxford University Press, 1979.

Leclerq, Victor. "Guillaume Duranti, Évêque de Mende, surnommé le Spéculateur." In *Histoire Littéraire de la France*, 20:411–80. Paris: Académie royale des Inscriptions et Belles-Lettres, 1895.

Lough, A. G. *John Mason Neale: Priest Extraordinary*. Devon: A. G. Lough, 1975.

Lubac, Henri de. *Exégèse médiévale: Les quatre sens de l'Écriture*. 2 vols. in 4 parts. Paris: Aubier, 1959–1964.

Ménard, Clarence C. "William Durand's *Rationale divinorum offciorum*: Preliminaries to a New Critical Edition." Ph.D. diss., Gregorian University, 1967.

Parker, Elizabeth C. "Architecture as Liturgical Setting." In *The Liturgy of the Medieval Church*, ed. Thomas J. Heffernan and E. Anne Matter, 273–326. Kalamazoo, Mich.: Medieval Institute Publications, 2001.

Pierce, Joanne M. "Vestments and Objects." In *The Oxford History of Christian Worship*, ed. Geoffrey Wainwright and Karen B. Westerfield Tucker, 841–57. Oxford: Oxford University Press, 2006.

Reynolds, Roger E. "Liturgy, Treatises on." *Dictionary of the Middle Ages* 7 (1986): 624–33.

Spatz, Nancy. "Church Porches and the Liturgy in Twelfth-Century Rome." In *The Liturgy of the Medieval Church*, ed. Thomas J. Heffernan and E. Anne Matter, 327–67. Kalamazoo, Mich.: Medieval Institute Publications, 2001.

Thibodeau, Timothy M. "Canon Law and Liturgical Exposition in Durand's *Rationale*." *Bulletin of Medieval Canon Law* 22 (1998): 41–52.

———. "The Doctrine of Transubstantiation in Durand's *Rationale*." *Traditio* 51 (1996): 308–17.

———. "*Enigmata Figurarum*: Biblical Exegesis and Liturgical Exposition in Durand's *Rationale*." *Harvard Theological Review* 86 (1993): 65–79.

———. "From Durand of Mende to St. Thomas More: Lessons Learned from Medieval Liturgy." In *Ritual, Text, and Law: Studies in Medieval Canon Law and Liturgy Presented to Roger E. Reynolds*, ed. Kathleen G. Cushing and Richard F. Gyug, 83–94. Aldershot: Ashgate, 2004.

———. "The Influence of Canon Law on Liturgical Exposition, c. 1100–1300." *Sacris Erudiri* 37 (1997): 185–202.

———. "Western Christendom." In *The Oxford History of Christian Worship*, ed. Geoffrey Wainwright and Karen B. Westerfield Tucker, 216–53. Oxford: Oxford University Press, 2006.

———. "William Durandus." In *Medieval Italy: An Encyclopedia*, ed. Christopher Kleinhenz, 2:1168–69. New York: Routledge, 2003.

Vogel, Cyrille. *Medieval Liturgy: An Introduction to the Sources.* Trans. and rev. W. G. Storey and N. K. Rasmussen. Washington, D.C.: The Pastoral Press, 1986.

Waley, Daniel. *The Papal State in the Thirteenth Century.* London: Macmillan, 1961.

Williman, J. P. "*Le racional de Divins Offices:* An Introduction and Partial Edition." Ph.D. diss., University of North Carolina, 1967.

INDEX